Trespassing

Trespassing

MY SOJOURN
IN THE
HALLS OF PRIVILEGE

Gwendolyn M. Parker

HOUGHTON MIFFLIN COMPANY

BOSTON · NEW YORK

1997

For information about permission to reproduce
selections from this book, write to Permissions,
Houghton Mifflin Company, 215 Park Avenue South,
New York, New York 10003.

Library of Congress Cataloging-in-Publication Data
Parker, Gwendolyn M.
Trespassing : my sojourn in the halls of privilege /
Gwendolyn M. Parker.
p.   cm.
ISBN 0-395-82297-1
1. Parker, Gwendolyn M. — Biography.   2. Afro-American
women novelists — 20th century — Biography.
3. Race relations — United States.   4. Middle class —
United States.   I. Title.
PS3566.A6786Z473   1997
813'.54 — dc21   [B]   97-19951   CIP

Printed in the United States of America

Book design by Robert Lowe

QUM 10 9 8 7 6 5 4 3 2 1

In memory of
Dr. Aaron McDuffie Moore
and the
Honorable John Bonner Duncan, Esq.,
for the continuing example
of their lives

Acknowledgments

Many thanks are due. First and foremost to my editor, Janet Silver, for encouraging me to tell this story; my agent, Marie Brown, whose efforts on my behalf always go far beyond the call of duty; my friend Joan, for patient listening, humor when needed, and thoughtful criticism; Mariella, for helping make the deadlines possible; Fatima and Sophie, for tea and sustenance; Marie and Ken of Lourie Lodge in South Africa, for four walls, a desk, and a view with flowers; Dawn, Nicole, Dan, Ronn, and K.C., for friendly support; my wild community of neighbors and friends — Alta, Kjell, Cathy, Margarett, and Moe — who helped with chores, lent me their cars, and offered fashion consults; and my four-year-old daughter, Lena, who, as she put it, "waited so nicely." And last, to the rest of my family — my mother, father, brothers, and ancestors — for allowing me to raid our collective lives.

Contents

Trespassing

PROLOGUE

Ghostly Remains

EVEN AS I WAS on the verge of letting it go, part of me still wanted to hang on. Not just to the obvious things, like the good money and the more than comfortable life that it purchased, but to the intangible of the persona, the identity itself. Even though I'd been wearing that identity more and more like a ghost, it still provided a measure of comfort, and cover: inside it, I was not left shifting about in my own naked skin. My protective covering also allowed me the option of hovering. I could always choose to be slightly above and apart. My particular costume was that of the accomplished black business professional. I wore it with a dash of cynicism cinched at the waist, but no amount of cynicism could undo the suit itself. It was carefully crafted.

I was wearing one of those well-tailored suits on that spring day in 1986 as I sat in the new corporate headquarters of the American Express Company at the World Financial Center, waiting to see the personnel officer with whom I'd made an appointment. She did not keep me waiting for long. Precisely at ten, she ushered me into her office, a small interior room with a solid wall instead of the smoky taupe glass partition that was standard issue for most middle-management offices in this new complex to which the company had moved just a few months before. The personnel officer and I knew each other, but not so well as to require prolonged pleasantries. It was therefore acceptable, after a few moments, for me to turn immediately to the subject at hand.

As she waited for me to begin, I had the briefest sensation of dislocation. It was not a wholly new sensation. For several weeks I'd had a similar feeling, as if I were set slightly apart. The refracted light in the office appeared to be causing everything in its ambit to change. The personnel officer's desk was not overly large, and as a result, we sat only a few feet from each other. She was quiet and still as she waited.

I suddenly wondered what my parents would say if they knew I was here. After all, these halls were my home now. I had sojourned for over ten years in them — centers of power and prestige in white America. I'd been trained in their very own breeding grounds, made my career at institutions that were still, at their pinnacles, overwhelmingly white and male. And though as a black female I was the perpetual outsider, persistently viewed as a trespasser on private preserves, at the same time it was a role I'd been groomed for since birth. I hailed from a small Southern town once described as the home of the black middle class, was the daughter of a pharmacist and a teacher, granddaughter to a banker and a businessman, great-granddaughter of a doctor who'd built one of the largest black-owned businesses. Ever since I left my cosseted Southern world, I'd honed my act as the first, or one of a handful, of blacks or women or both. Along with one other black girl, I integrated an exclusive boarding school, Kent, in Connecticut.

With a few other black women I represented my race at Radcliffe College in the turbulent 1960s. Mine was the sole black female face at the conservative white-shoe Wall Street firm Cadwalader, Wickersham & Taft. And during my eight years at American Express, as a director, I'd been among a handful of blacks and women straining toward senior management. Where I was now was where all of the familial expectations had led. Still, I had not told my parents, nor any of my family except one of my brothers, what I'd planned. And though it had been all that I'd thought of for weeks, now that the moment had come, I still couldn't believe it. Nevertheless, I'd done nothing irrevocable. I could make up another reason for this meeting. I did not, in fact, have to utter any of the words I'd rehearsed so carefully.

"I have had a good career here with American Express," I began, and that much was true. On the surface of things, I certainly had no cause to complain. Since I'd joined the company nearly eight years before, the promotions had come at a fast-track pace, each one, up until this last job, in less than two years. I had been named a Black Achiever in Industry. I had been in departments that were the envy of many of my colleagues, working, for example, on the highly visible Shearson acquisition. I was even on a first-name basis with some of the most senior people in the company.

"And throughout my years here, one thing was always consistent — I was always treated fairly."

This was also primarily true. True on the level of personal choice, true of the stated and best of intentions. But as the years had gone by, I'd been forced to confront again and again the limits of merely evenhanded treatment. Treating me fairly did not change the yardstick by which I was judged. It did not alter the standards to which I was held. It did not transform me, in one iota, from a constant exception to the general rule. Nothing, in fact, about the treatment of me changed the habits, predilections, and foundations that made this company the institution it was, with the values that formed and sustained it, values that mirrored my own in many places, and diverged as sharply in other places as the currents that had formed each of us went where no one could touch them, underground. In all the meetings I'd participated in, I'd thought of myself as just a slim brown face pulling up to the table, prepared like everyone else to meet the task at hand. But my brownness, my femaleness, my unexpected competence, even the surprising fact of my middle-class status, could not help but confound a culture that thinks it knows who I am, and where I should be, and is ever threatened when I turn up where I'm least expected.

"Fairness has been important to me," I continued, and that much was also accurate, how the level of personal intention had been both a balm and a distraction, blinding me to the realities of how far personal intentions might go.

"Now all I'm asking is that the company continue to do the same."

The personnel officer was well trained, with a natural affinity for her work. She did not have to bite her lip to keep from interrupting me, or grip the side of the desk, as I had seen one senior manager do during a mandated person-to-person chat, his personality as unsuited to passive listening as mine was to the sarcasm that was his real forte.

She did not say anything, and for a few moments neither

did I. Though I had imagined myself as ready, no planning was adequate preparation for diving, without checking, into a bottomless quarry. Yet that was just what I felt I was about to do — about to cast off with one impulsive plunge a whole lifetime of training, education, and grooming, and for what? For something certainly my parents, if they had known, would describe as a whim.

Ever since the idea had come to me — to quit my job in order to write — it was all I could think of. I wanted to try and turn the turmoil and chaos that had gripped my department the previous year to my advantage, and emerge jobless but with a cushion of five to six months' severance pay. I had turned the scenario over in my mind countless times. My hope that a six-month buffer might solve anything — that I would be anywhere, much less where I wanted and needed to be, in so short a time — may have been wholly fanciful, but it gave me courage and grit, just the smallest bit of insulation from reality that I needed.

"My whole staff has been let go," I continued. "I haven't had a budget, or really even a job, for over six months. It's as though I have been let go. It seems only fair that I be given a settlement package."

This turn took the personnel officer completely by surprise. When I'd set up the meeting, I imagined she'd expect a list of grievances, demands about the new job I'd been told about; she'd probably planned to reassure me about my new place on the team. That I wanted out altogether hadn't been part of what she'd envisioned.

"But you are one of the people we want to keep," she said, sounding genuinely startled. "We want you as part of the new team. You will be an important player. I think you know how much we value your contribution."

"Thank you, I've always felt that. And that's why I'm hoping you will be fair with me now."

From there on out, we simply repeated ourselves — she, to be sure she understood what I was asking; I, to give her the line I wanted to be repeated to her superiors. She wants out, with a package, she would tell them. I think she's unhappy with the new boss — who was an old colleague of mine — coming in over her. I don't see any real legal exposure, but she is well liked by people. She's been a team player, and we are, after all, trying to put the past behind us. I don't see a problem with giving her a package, I hoped she would say.

I could see the personnel officer assaying me, trying to calculate my motives. Though I had carefully thought out the mechanics and strategy of my departure, what was driving me was totally unrelated to reason. How, I wondered, could I ever explain a decision propelled by motives as insubstantial as breath: a belief that I had something more to offer than an increase in the bottom line, a notion that my life was supposed to have meaning, a desire to just go, get out, seize back the life that I'd bartered away.

Despite the familiar script of success, this present was not where my past should have led. And from the moment I yielded to that, something ancient took over. Bequeathing a conviction — in the absence of fact — that things would somehow work out in the end. Deeding a belief that I could even do what it was I was hoping to do. Buoying me up with wild faith and a willingness to leap. And leap is just what I did at last. Out of bonuses and yearly increases. Out of a decade-long career that afforded fortnightly dinners at Lutèce and yearly vacations in the south of France. Out of my well-worn corporate shape into something that was wholly unknown. I awaited for months a final decision. After my initial meeting, I met with several different people in Personnel. I was cool and calm and rational. All the while, something else was pressing me toward an opening that I'd suddenly spied. And all of it — the jockeying for power and position, the barriers I always met and the things that enabled me to smooth the way — fell behind. I was untethered, a balloon set loose, flying free on my way toward my past.

ONE

Cloistered in a Colored World

*F*OR THAT long stretch of memory that is childhood, colored people were all that I knew. They were compass and referent, copper, beige, pecan brown.

The place was Durham, North Carolina, a small segregated Southern town, extolled by virtue of its thriving black community as the black Wall Street and the home of the black middle class. The accomplishments of Durham's Negro citizens were held up everywhere as a model of racial relations and proof of the vitality of the American dream. The country's largest black business was there, and that business — the North Carolina Mutual Life Insurance Company, founded at the turn of the century — along with the many institutions that were fostered by the Mutual and its leaders, served as a magnet to members of the black intelligentsia, race leaders, prominent entertainers, and politicians who were constantly in circulation in the town.

Though I was unaware of this public face, it was part and parcel of the Durham that I first knew and loved as a child. I was part of the postwar baby boom, born in June of 1950, the only girl among two boys: Garrett, who was less than two years my senior, and Tony, who followed me by five years. As a social class, we Durham colored were somewhat unique: an

upper and middle class that was entrepreneurial in nature and
that had not been wholly wedded to color distinctions at its
birth. Ours was a community that in the 1940s and 1950s
boasted a higher percentage of home ownership by colored
people than anywhere else in the nation, a community of relentlessly self-serving as well as race-serving men and women.
It was a community with intricate and at times ambivalent ties
to the larger white community, ties that resulted in a boom
in factory jobs for blacks in the burgeoning tobacco industry
and led to the founding of a hospital for coloreds, Lincoln.
The backroom deal for the hospital was struck at the turn of
the century, with my great-grandfather supposedly bargaining
for the seed money with a member of the Duke family who
originally planned to erect a monument in memory of the
mammy who had cared for his family. It was also a community
that figured symbolically in the early-twentieth-century debates between W. E. B. Du Bois and Booker T. Washington,
with its ruling elite an example of the "talented tenth" Du Bois
called upon to do what they could for the race, and its material
progress the type that Washington believed would represent
the Negro's salvation.

This was the Durham that formed the backdrop to my
young life. I didn't realize that grinding poverty in towns not
nearly so fortunate as Durham was the lot of so many of my
people. Nor, as a young child, did I realize how very lucky I
was. I didn't ponder the meaning of the heritage I was born to,
I simply took advantage of its succor, and at the same time
indulged myself in what all children indulge themselves in
initially — namely, the sensory and familial world into which
they are born.

My parents were a natural force. My father was an outgoing, charming, stubbornly independent man, hugely attractive by all accounts to the opposite sex, blessed with a mind that was facile and quick, a man with an easygoing manner punctured at times by inexplicable bursts of temper. My earliest recollections of him are of those outbursts as well as the great delight he took in my spirit and drive. My mother was an earthy, sensuous, bright, beautiful woman, temperamentally conservative, who took great delight in her home and her children. My earliest memories of her are of the rich creamy tone and warmth of her skin and of the alternating flashes of anger and spells of depression to which she was prey. Both she and my father had an electric will, and living with them was sometimes like being in the midst of a gathering storm. I inherited their combined will, my mother's lean frame, her height and high cheekbones, and my father's brown skin, his stubbornness, and his quick mind. Though my parents and I would later skirmish, and though their tempers sometimes frightened me, my most persistent memories are of a world that was predominantly welcoming.

It was a world defined by heat: the Durham summers were hot and muggy and extended from April to October, and the winters were mild and brief. The outdoors, in the form of screened porches and stoops that sloped away to large manicured lawns, was a part of my daily round of experience, and for a child enamored of the sensual world, as I was, it was a propitious place to live. I lolled, boundless, in its sweaty embrace. Light and shadow, the majestic swoop of the trees, the sharp grit of dirt, the smooth coolness of breezes drifting through screens, all of these propelled me through my earliest days. I took from them my first concept of meaning and pattern, and I had no doubts about my certain place within nature's ordered beauty.

When I looked beyond the natural world, I felt similarly cosseted. I lived in an entire neighborhood of family, relatives to the north, south, east, and west of me, all up and down our block of tidy brick homes. Perched on the hill behind us was the large house of my mother's mother, Grandmother McDougald, our back yards flowing from one to the other like one huge playground. Next to us were one set of my mother's first cousins and their children, and beyond them another set of first cousins. And every door was always open to me. Most mornings I took a second breakfast with my grandmother McDougald of raisin toast slathered with sweet butter and as much bacon as we both cared to eat while my grandmother's housekeeper, Lucille, told us news of the neighborhood. Cousin Pearl next door was always good for fresh lemonade, the pulp and sugar dancing across my tongue as Cousin Pearl delivered some admonition or warning in her gravelly voice to which I would only half attend. Throughout the neighborhood, I listened at doors, sat at knees, pulled up to tables for a drink, a snack, or a meal, or just sat and chattered a minute. "Gwennie Mac, come on in," someone would say as I peered through a screen door to see what was happening inside. I would sit down to whatever meal was in progress, another slim brown face at the table, eyes peeping out from a face framed by wild pigtails. There was no home that was closed to me, no doors that I could not open. Everywhere I turned, life was an unqualified yes.

The only task with which I was charged as a child was to do my best, whatever I did. This exhortation toward excellence was impressed upon me not only as a personal mandate but as the lifeblood that had created the town. If the words themselves were not ground up and fed to me with my morning grits, they might as well have been.

All of Durham, in fact, white as well as black, had been cobbled together by self-made men, with the tobacco-rich Dukes at the top. But for us colored (what we called ourselves then), descended from farmers and country people, being the best was infused with an added dimension — it was almost a holy defense. It was the first line of protection against a world that sometimes refused to be tamed. Being the best was a strong, high fence to keep intruders out and the family in; it was the sturdy plow that turned over the ground and the tightly woven basket used to gather the grain; it was the schoolhouse to which, no matter how far away, we could always walk.

The colored people I was born to were hard workers, because working hard was what they had learned from their parents. They were hard workers no matter their station in life, and if they were fortunate, then they felt it their righteous duty to work all the harder. They were also zealots when it came to the difference that education could make, and they used both land and education to leverage and garner the other. They saw the fruits of their labor, believed in the efficacy of their own will and that a better day was coming. It was the Puritan ethic enlivened by racial reality.

Culturally we were all colored, though in the realm of biology, like most colored we were a diverse lot. My maternal grandfather was light enough, with wavy brown hair, to pass for white when he chose to. My paternal great-grandfather was a dark-brown-skinned man who had been born a slave. We counted African, Scottish, Cherokee, and Tuscarora among our heritage, and before the passage of laws that prevented it, some of the white ancestors had married African or African–Native American women, and bequeathed land to the potpourri of children that were left behind. One of my ancestors was rumored to have been a Scottish pirate, one of two brothers who took up farming in an area far outside of town. From the one brother who took a mixed African–Native American woman as his wife came many of my mother's relatives; from the other brother came the McDougalds — my mother's family name — who were all white.

This heritage belonged to everyone who lived in Durham, but I was made to know that it carried a special meaning for me. And that was because I was not just the only daughter of Yip Parker and Arona Moore McDougald, but because I was also, on my father's side, the granddaughter of Beatrice Burnett Parker, founder of the first Youth Council of the NAACP, and on my mother's side the granddaughter of R. L. McDougald and the great-granddaughter of Aaron McDuffie Moore, cofounder of the North Carolina Mutual Life Insurance Company. I learned that I had inherited not only physical attributes and temperament, but had been bequeathed habits of thought and belief as well. I realized, in fact, as soon as I knew it, that there was scarcely a conscious moment of my life when I couldn't recite every detail of my family history.

My mother's father and grandfather loomed particularly large in this heritage. The legacies of their lives were everywhere evident in the town, and though they had died long before I was born, they were talked about as if they were just temporarily absent: "Your great-grandfather, he would do or say thus and so." Even those who had known my great-grandfather quite well would always use his title, to denote respect: "Dr. Moore, when he was alive, this wouldn't have happened." People would peer at me and my two brothers, looking for signs of him: "Your brother Tony, he's the spitting image of your great-grandfather. Look at that child." Or say to me, "You've got that long look, just like Dr. Moore."

The list of my great-grandfather's accomplishments was legend. With one of his close friends, John Merrick, he started the Mutual, for many years the largest colored-owned business in the country. He became a doctor at the age of twenty-five, placing second in the state medical exam. He was a founder of the first colored hospital in Durham and was instrumental in the growth of many of the city's key institutions, including the White Rock Baptist Church, the Stanford Warren Library, the Mechanics and Farmers Bank, and North Carolina Central University. He had helped lay the groundwork for an entrepreneurial empire, but more than that, he was a man with a vision and a mission. The Mutual was, as he perceived it, not only a place to earn money. It was an institution charged with the uplift and betterment of his people. Should God and Mammon collide, he had always made it clear: let Mammon go.

People loved to tell stories about his generosity. They talked about how he would tend a patient in exchange for a pig, or if there was no pig, in exchange for nothing at all. Young people from "down country" who showed promise came to live in his Durham home, and in exchange for some chores were put through school. He kept extra shoes and spare clothes in a back closet to give to anyone who needed them for church. He was not only a doctor, a businessman, and a philosopher, according to those who knew him intimately, but also a deeply spiritual man.

My favorite picture of him hung in the halls of the new North Carolina Mutual building, but I had first seen it in the home of my great-aunt Lyda, his daughter. The portrait showed a man with a slender, gentle face, a graceful forehead, and huge, protruding ears that seemed to temper features that otherwise might have been too handsome. I remember thinking that he was a remarkable-looking man — remarkable because of the beauty of his face, but even more so because of the look in his eyes. His gaze was direct and self-confident without being aggressive or cocky. He looked intelligent, but it was an intelligence touched by something else, a wisdom, and a feeling that he was at peace with himself. I thought of him as a secret friend, someone who, as I gazed back at him, was delivering his secrets only to me.

It was a long time before I realized that the great-grandfather spoken of with such awe and love and reverence was this very same man, my secret protector and guide. Once I knew that they were one and the same, he assumed almost mythic proportions. I never tired of hearing stories about him. He became the icon to which I would refer any action. I always asked myself what he would think, and that's what I would seek to achieve.

My grandfather, on the other hand, was a more robust and earthly presence. People did not speak of R. L. McDougald in the hushed tones reserved for Aaron McDuffie Moore. They did not lean down to get close to me when they wanted to tell me something about him. Instead, they threw their heads back, laughed, and slapped their knees or smacked their lips. Mac they called him. "Mac," they would say, "he sure did pull a fast one." "Remember that Packard Mac liked to drive? If Mac were here, he'd know how to make some money off of that." From what I could tell, Mac too was outsized, though not so much in compassion as in smarts and business savvy and humor and temper. He made a ton of money, and made it fast. People looked up to him and feared him. Had he lived past the age of forty-six, when the drive that propelled him finally burst his heart, there was no telling how far he might have gone. He had been the executive vice president of the Mechanics and Farmers Bank. He developed numerous real estate projects for the bank, the most prominent of which, called McDougald Terrace, a housing tract for the rising colored working class, was completed after his death. He was on the board of the Mutual, and he owned land and single-family homes all around town. Supposedly he kept a safe full of money, and it was reportedly that money that my grandmother, his young widow, used to build the grand brick house she lived in, perched up on the corner of Lawson Street right behind our house, the house that, for so many years after her death, figured in my dreams.

This effect of recognizing my place in the constellation of the town was forceful: it not only formed the boundaries of my past, it also outlined the direction in which I was expected to go. These expectations were a beacon and a compass, and also a bedrock of values. Whatever deeds were accomplished, it was the meaning of those deeds that mattered: Progress for the race. Being the first. Opening doors for those who will come behind. Making our people proud. I lived in a town that had historic dimensions for our people, and the people who had

built the institutions that gave the city its titles were my ancestors.

These were the voices from the past, but there were living
daily reminders as well. Right across the street from my grandmother's house was North Carolina Central, the college for the
colored that my great-grandfather had helped foster and that
the Mutual had in its early years supported. My mother taught
mathematics there, and students from the college were my
babysitters. In the afternoons, I would look out my grandmother's library window as they made their way from their
classes to their dorms. Almost everyone in my parents' circle
had a college degree, and many, like my parents, had a master's
or more. My mother had earned her master's in math education from Columbia; my father had his pharmacist's degree
from Philadelphia College of Pharmacy. So for all of my time
growing up, it was a given that I would go on to some form of
graduate school. Similarly with things of the spirit: we went to
church on most Sundays. We said grace before most of our
meals. Though neither of my parents was particularly devout, a
belief in something larger than oneself was taken for granted.
Likewise with business: it was considered both intimate and
essential. My father was a pharmacist with his own store in
the center of the colored business district, and his uncle was
also a pharmacist with his own store, as was my great-aunt.
Even the accomplishments of my ancestors were concrete living presences: houses to live in; streets like the ones in McDougald Terrace that I could walk down and were named after
my mother and her two sisters; a thriving institution like the
Mutual, where colored men and women from all over the
country still came with high hopes for a job.

Even more salient to me as a child was the way the values

instilled in me were interconnected. There was no teasing one thread away from another: people needed to be fed and housed and clothed, they needed education, they needed insurance to care for their own after death. All of these things had value, all required their servants, and the many different needs of the community flowed as effortlessly from one side of the street to the other as I did as a child.

While the close-knit and interbred nature of Durham provided a fertile hothouse environment for a child, the overwrought nature of the town did not appeal to all sensibilities. My father, for one, seemed particularly to dislike the glare of intense interest. By contrast, I liked the fact that everyone knew everyone else, and that everyone's comings and goings were a matter of note. I especially liked the constant flow of talk that was so much a part of my day. I loved the way women's voices rose and fell when they greeted each other. "Girlllllll," they would trill, "how you been?" The "been" an emphatic smack. I loved the rumble of the men's voices, pitched low but also secretive, so that the children — and the women too, I suspected — would not overhear. When people came out of church, the sudden chatter was like an explosion, all the quiet and decorum of our middle-class congregation dispelled. People swirled together, eager to hear all the news, and I swirled with them, first in this group, then in that. A few doors away, at my father's drugstore, people would gather for ice cream, pick up prescriptions, and continue the talk, heads bobbing, bodies leaning toward each other confidentially. I liked to duck behind the long mahogany counter or hide in the back room, where the prescriptions were mixed, and listen from there.

"She thinks nobody notices, but Flora saw her. Hmmph. Tippytoeing. Like she thinks she's somebody grand."

Or, "And did you hear how she went on? All of that talk about money. Does she think she's the only one with a foxtail? I've had plenty of foxtails in my life!"

"Umm-hmm," someone might add. "And that silly fur coat. Who needs a fur coat if you don't travel. And when was the last time they went anywhere?"

"And you know why, don't you? Because Harold is cheap, cheap, cheap."

Cheap or bossy or tippytoeing, or too fond of Wild Turkey, or caught in her housecoat after twelve o'clock. Stellar hostesses and people whose homes were so dirty that their housekeeper quit. Brilliant dealmakers with rude and unmannerly children. Best friends who no longer spoke to each other. This one or that one who hadn't a flaw.

From my eavesdropping I began to recognize allegiances, loyalties, rankings, and with this recognition came the beginning of what I viewed as my coming awake. Up until then, I had taken reality as all of a piece, with no part separated out from the rest. It was not ordered or arranged, but merely existed without hierarchy. Now I began to see that the world was not all a seamless whole, that instead there were places and spaces, that people could tumble out of favor, that even within this tightly knit world there was the constant threat of a precipitous fall.

And yet, despite the sharp talk, I was surprised to learn that no one was ever exiled. Poor Miss So-and-so could be talked about like the devil before she arrived and after she left, but she was invited every week, just the same. My father would decry this habit as the height of hypocrisy, but to me as a child, it became a comfort. It said that no matter how grave the transgression, no member would ever be cast out of the tribe.

After my parents, and the ancestors who were long gone, my grandmothers had the greatest influence on my childhood. My maternal and paternal grandmothers were like two contrasting bookends girding opposite sides of our proper, Southern, colored middle-class life. While my maternal grandmother was the ultimate arbiter of good taste, decorum, and propriety, my paternal grandmother reigned over the educational and political realm. They each had their assigned roles, and each took her position quite seriously.

My grandmother McDougald was a tiny wren of a woman who spent most of the lifetime in which I knew her laboriously and earnestly making her nest. From the money my grandfather had made in his short life, my grandmother McDougald lived on and lived well, never working a day in her life after her marriage to him. Her first move a few years after his death was to build herself a grand house, for her occupancy alone. It had a large, modern kitchen, a formal dining room and living room, a large second-story screened-in porch, a library, an entryway dominated by a spiral staircase and crystal chandelier, and an upstairs with three large bedrooms, each equipped with a bath. She bought the choicest of furniture and clothes, and furnished her home to be the envy of everyone in Durham. I can only imagine now what it must have been like for her, a schoolteacher from a small town in New Jersey, transported south as Mr. Mac's new bride, stepmother to two young girls grieving for their own mother, and then two years later, mother to her own young daughter. But however it was for her inside, on the outside my grandmother McDougald wore the mantle of business scion's widow well. She never remarried. She spent her husband's money with taste and great pleasure. She owned a shiny car, buying a new one every two or so years. She didn't know how to drive, but she had a man to drive for her, so that she would never have to suffer the indignity of riding in the back of a public bus. She went on cruises in the winter, and, after we moved to the North, shopped at Saks Fifth Avenue, where she sat amid the designer clothes, and salesladies brought out to her whatever she wanted to look at.

When I was older, we would go to Schrafft's in New York City for lunch and have chicken sandwiches with the crusts cut off. For the train ride home from the city we would buy Fannie Farmer chocolates and walnut fudge. My grandmother liked her sherry in a crystal glass, her lamb chops trimmed just so. Her living room was filled with gleaming mahogany furniture, Hummel figurines, doilies, and velvet brocade loveseats and couches. From her I learned that if you are lucky enough to have money, no one can force you to accept second best, that money gives you freedom that not even white people can take away. You could put down your money and escape to the sun whenever you chose. You could shop in the stores, or at least in the catalogues, that you wanted. You could go to restaurants in the North and eat all of the lobster and shrimp that you wanted.

She was a tasteful, conservative, unabashed sensualist. She never went to extremes, but she never apologized for loving and enjoying beautiful things, for appreciating a well-cooked meal, a well-stitched leather glove, a well-made piece of furniture. With her, I was the sensualist as well. She bought me expensive Italian gloves lined with fur (which my parents said I was sure to lose, but which I held on to until they were frayed) and gold-leaf-embossed books that she knew I would cherish. I swooned with delight in her library, with its glass-fronted mahogany bookcases, three walls of beautiful books, and overstuffed chairs.

There were many like my grandmother McDougald in Durham, people who took deep pleasure from their material possessions. Cars were a special source of pride. When I turned nine, my parents bought a pink and white Lincoln, the same color as the bike I got that year, and we drove it slowly around town like eager peacocks. When my cousin Pearl and her husband, Ulysses, got new living room furniture, everyone was invited over to see it. Easter Sunday was an orgy of new dresses and shiny patent-leather shoes and handbags, the display of them in morning church inevitably followed by afternoon calls to show them off some more. To me it was an indivisible whole, this love of things both tangible and invisible. People cheerfully mixed the spiritual and the mundane, and I did as well.

At the opposite end of the spectrum sat my grandmother Parker, Miss Bea as she was known to all. Scratch any Southern colored family and you find a woman like her. She was the churchgoing, organizing, tireless social activist who would never take no for an answer. For most of her life, like others of her ilk, she kept up a range of activities with dizzying energy. She taught English and math and social studies and physical education for over fifty years. She was a feminist before anyone else was even thinking of using the word, a staunch believer that a girl or a woman was the equal of any boy or man, and to prove it, she organized sports for the girls when the school provided none. She taught Sunday school and was one of the founders of her church and its oldest member. She organized the first Youth Council of the NAACP. She was for seventeen years the president of her local NAACP chapter and traveled every year, no matter the distance, to the national convention. She had her own opinion about anything and everything, and was never afraid to express it. In fact, she could talk your ear off, nonstop, day or night, if she was in the mood, and if you tried to get away, she would grasp you with a grip so tight that you feared she might snap off your arm. Grandmother Parker was stalwart, robust, talkative, aggressive, and too much for anybody to live with, so after two brief marriages she lived alone, in the sleepy town of Tarboro, next to her sister Mattie, who never married and ran the local drugstore. Miss Bea lived to be 102.

I learned many things from her, particularly once I was old enough to piece things together for myself. It was from her that I took my first intimations of class and expanded upon it. Down the street from her lived the first family that I recognized as poor, a family of at least a dozen children living in a huge, shambling white house. Every Saturday night in the summer, with my less than able assistance, my grandmother made pots of greens, large trays of corn bread, buckets of rice and black-eyed peas, and a huge pot of some sort of meat — smothered pork chops, perhaps, or stewing beef, but meat, and a lot of it. We would eat our small amount and then she would ring a bell out in the back yard, and one of the children who

lived in that white house would come running. My grandmother would tell her to go ask her mother if she would do
Miss Bea a favor.

"I cooked way too much food," she would tell the child,
then nod at me. "This young 'un eats like a bird. Ask your
mother if she would be so kind as to help me keep all this food
from wasting. If she wouldn't mind, you and a few of your
brothers and sisters come back with some pots."

A few minutes later the oldest child would return with a
gaggle of recruits behind her, each carrying a battered pot or
chipped bowl. "Miss Bea," the oldest would say, "my mother
says she would be glad to help you. You can just put what's the
leftovers in these pots and bowls." Then my grandmother
would ladle out as much as she could, and the children would
depart like a ragtag platoon, the pots and bowls hugged to their
chests, up close to their noses.

Gestures like these were frequent and went without comment, but I took from them a new awareness. Children who
before had simply lived or dressed differently from me now
were something else: they were in need — of food or clothes
— and my grandmother assumed it was our role to provide.

Grandmother Parker might have been gentle with these
children, but it was about the only way she was gentle. She was
a proud, feisty woman, with a memory so keen that she loved
to show off. She could remember the full name of every one of
the thousands of children she had taught. And not only their
names, but their brothers' and sisters' and parents' names too.
She was forever running into former students — "Miss Bea,
Miss Bea, do you remember me?" — and she would proudly
call them by name and ask about their parents and each one of

their siblings. "Taught her in the third grade," she'd say to me later. "She moved away in the fifth. Her father lost his job in a factory, and just two years ago she moved back. She has two little girls now of her own."

My grandmother's pride in her memory was part and parcel of the value she placed on things of the mind. In her book, smart was the best and absolute best you could be. "Little Ginny So-and-so," she would say, "smart as a whip. Harry Turner, now there was a boy who was smart! Mr. Roy Wilkins, as smart as they come." She would tell me stories about how bright my father had been as a boy, going off to college at fifteen, learning subjects in half or a quarter the time that it took somebody else. "Now this young 'un," she would say when I accompanied her around town, laying her hand on my shoulder and pushing me forward, "now she's just as smart, maybe smarter than her father." Then she would relate some tale about how young I had been when I started to read, how good my grades were, that as a baby I had started to talk not in single words, according to her, but in full sentences.

As I listened more carefully, I learned that to Grandmother Parker intelligence was a weapon, a sharp, infinitely useful instrument, good for dealing with anyone but especially with white folks, who, as she put it, never expected colored people to have any brains.

I heard about white people throughout my young years, but I really didn't know who they were. The world I lived in was strictly segregated. I went to a colored school, shopped in colored stores, went to the colored movie theater near my father's drugstore. The white people my grandmother Parker talked about were usually related to some story in the past that she told, so I assumed they were particular people she had known in Tarboro and disliked. Whenever she spoke of them, it was with disdain or in a haughty tone. By contrast, when I heard white people mentioned at home, it was sometimes in a very offhand way — that someone had run into some white people who did thus and so. I decided that "white people" was a great catchall that could and did mean different things depending on who said it, in the same way that "blue" coming out of different mouths could mean so many different things. One meaning of "white people," I gathered, was that it actually did refer to skin color, and so I decided that all of the light-skinned people I knew were white. This included my mother, my grandmother McDougald, my aunt Julia, my cousin Constance and her husband, Charles, and some number — I wasn't sure how many — of their children. Jane Johnson, my best friend who lived up the street, in this scheme was also white.

But the word "white" had no meaning beyond this description — it was simply a means of pinpointing a physical fact. Though other meanings doubtless swirled about me, I was oblivious of them. Years later, I would read something that my grandmother Parker had said about white people and the colored's relationship, as she had known it, to them. "I have never taken low," she said. "I'm as good as the President. The President has one vote, and I have one vote." And in her resolve and determination she was fearless. "Nothing is going to stop me," she was quoted as saying, "especially where my people are concerned. I am not afraid of anything."

TWO

Northern Exposure

JUST A FEW WEEKS before my ninth birthday, our family left Durham for good. My father sold his pharmacy business, we sold our house to a cousin, and my mother left her job as a math teacher at the college. We were moving north, to a place called Mount Vernon, New York — at that time, 1959, a quiet suburb of New York City, home for many years to scores of Italians, Irish, and Jews looking for tree-lined streets to raise their children, and increasingly a destination for blacks from the South or from New York City seeking the same. It was the town where the Delaney sisters — who would later go on to fame for their book *Having Our Say* — lived (around the corner from where we eventually bought a house), and where my mother's oldest sister, her husband, and their three children already lived.

The move was wholly my father's idea. As he later confessed, he had never wanted to be a pharmacist (he had only reluctantly followed in the footsteps of his uncle and aunt, both pharmacists with their own stores), and he neither enjoyed the long hours his work as a pharmacist and store owner required nor took any great pleasure in the work itself. I think too that as a fiercely independent man he despised the small-town atmosphere of Durham. He was tired of being Yip, the nickname by which he was known — Miss Bea's boy, who was married to one of the McDougald sisters. Always a bit of a rebel, with his own ideas about how things should be done, he also wanted, I think, to finally break free of the net of relationships that to us children felt like welcome support and helped define us, but that to a young man must have felt like a yoke.

For the year before the move, my father had been away at Michigan State, working on a graduate degree in psychology, so that once we were in New York he could begin his new chosen career. When he had his first job lined up as a children's counselor at the New York City Juvenile Detention Center, we were ready to go.

Though the impending move, and my father's absence that had preceded it, had been uppermost in my mind for the better part of a year, it never seemed quite real to me that we might leave all that I'd known for good. I told people eagerly about our move, was proud of the fact that we were doing what was not frequently done, but I thought of it simply as a great adventure, and in my mind, when the adventure was over, I fully expected that we would return. Besides, the North was an impossible place. It was where people went for weekend excursions, returning with souvenir matchbooks and embossed ashtrays showing the Statue of Liberty. It was where the musicians on jazz albums lived. It was even an explanation for inexplicable behavior: that someone was from the North explained what otherwise could not be understood. People said the words in capital letters: that happened UP NORTH, those people are from UP NORTH.

My father spoke of our destination with equal parts relief and reverence. He seemed more than eager to go. We would find things undreamed of there; we would be delivered of some chafing restrictions. The schools will be so much better up north, I heard him say. The children will have opportunities there they could never have here. Even more urgently, he argued, they will have opportunities there that we never had.

At the time, I did not know of the constraints of which my father spoke. My life had been sheltered, and within its secure walls I felt free, and I could not imagine that the world could be any better. Nevertheless, I was excited simply by his excitement, and moved by the thrill of the new and unknown. I tried to envision the limitless world he described, but whenever I tried to form a picture, all I could see was a vague place mysteriously pulsing. I imagined that the people there looked like the people on my father's jazz albums, sitting in blue-lit places, music relentlessly pounding, with nighttime the only time. My only concrete information about the North was that it was big, and people spoke differently there. I had met people from the North and been instantly taken by their speech, sassy and bold. They did not dawdle over their words; instead, they spoke as if time was scurrying by. Their words were crisp and clipped, and they were judicious in the use of their hands. No long trills or whoops or glides. If someone's name was Sue, they called her Sue, not *S-uu-u,* in three syllables as a Southerner said it. I imagined that I would no longer be Gwennie Mac, since there would be no neighbor up the street named Gwen Green from whom I would need to be distinguished, and besides, saying it would take up too much time. I would probably be known as just Gwen.

So I made myself ready. I listened carefully to how Northerners spoke and then I swallowed their speech in a furious gulp. Before we'd even left home, in early summer, people said I was starting to talk funny. By the time we reached our destination, I'd tossed my Southern accent out somewhere on the side of the road.

I wanted to stay awake the whole trip. The back seat of our Lincoln was filled with blankets and pillows and food and boxes, but I was determined not to sink into its comfort and fall asleep. Twilight turned quickly to darkness and we began to pick up far-flung stations on the radio. My parents double-checked route numbers and landmarks as one road changed seamlessly into another. Occasionally we passed another lone car, but for long stretches of road we saw only our own headlights, and no matter how hard I fought it, sleep would not be put off any longer. When I finally awoke early the next morning, it was to learn that we had arrived. We turned off a narrow highway and were suddenly in a warren of streets shrouded on both sides by thick green foliage. This was what I first noticed: the color of the trees, a darker green than the variety of trees in the South, and the street, cast in deeper shade. There were houses hidden behind the green, set back a discreet distance from the street. It was as if they had pulled back just a bit, claiming greater privacy for themselves. We turned and turned and turned again, and I feared we were lost, until we climbed a steep hill at the crest of which we came to a stop.

My mother said, "Four-twelve McClellan, this is it." We stumbled sleepily out of the car. In front of us was a large house with a big front porch and maroon shutters. It rose up before me at such a pitched angle that it was hard to see all of it without throwing my head way back, and when I did that, I nearly got dizzy. Coming down the steep porch steps were my aunt and my cousins, greeting us as my father began to pile what seemed like all of our belongings onto the street.

I had met my mother's older sister, my aunt Virginia — Ginn as she was called — maybe once or twice before in my life, and what I had most remembered about her was her great rush of energy. That same energy flew to us now. "Gwennie Mac, Little Garrett, Tony, Arona, Garrett," she said, hugging us in quick succession. She squeezed, released, looked each of us up and down as if checking for breakage, and then went on to the next. She had wiry thick hair that crackled around her head and eyes that darted about as quickly as hummingbirds' wings. She was an organizer to beat all organizers. This was to go here, that was to go there. Little Garrett, you can carry that over there. She took all of us and our stuff in hand and directed it hither and yon, and within seconds, it seemed, it was swallowed up by her huge high house. I was installed on the second floor with my cousin Ginga, eight years my senior; Garrett and Tony were stowed somewhere on the third floor; and my parents were down the hall from me in a big square room next to the bathroom. Somewhere in the midst of the confusion, I was introduced to my aunt Ginn's husband, Ed Warren O'Daniel, whom all of the grownups called O'D. Uncle Eddie I called him. He was a tall, handsome man with wonderfully smooth brown skin and soft curly hair that he wore slicked down, long for a man, so that it ended in a series of curls at his collar. I gave him a shy hug. He looked down at me and laughed a long laugh.

"So this is the infamous Gwennie Mac," he said, surveying me with great amusement. "Girl, after all the stories I heard about you, I thought you were going to have horns."

I didn't have time to ponder what those stories might be, because we were all hustled into the kitchen, where pots the size of which I'd never seen before sat on the stove.

"I know you all must be hungry," my aunt Ginn said, directing us toward the food and some plates.

I was soon to learn that food — and vast quantities of it — played a major role in my cousins' lives. No sooner would one meal be over than preparations for the next would begin. I would grow to hate the day it was my turn to do the dishes, a stint that usually lasted several hours before every ten-gallon pot was clean.

Though we would live with my aunt and uncle and my three cousins — Ricky, Ginga, and Eddie — until we found a house of our own, which took nearly a year, I never grew totally accustomed to living with them. The sheer quantity of food my cousins consumed was only one among myriad mysteries about them. Ginga was seventeen, a lifetime away, it seemed, and I wondered endlessly about her life and was grateful for the smallest scrap of attention. Even Eddie and Ricky, only twelve and fourteen, in their sophistication seemed so much older than my brother Garrett and me. All three cousins were always coming and going. They each seemed as busy as my aunt, and if they weren't out of the house, some friend or friends of theirs were invited over. Eddie harmonized with an a cappella group in the front parlor. Ricky debated politics in the kitchen. Ginga was at her sewing machine with friends in her room. The house was as busy as if two dozen of us lived there, and the air was constantly filled with talk and music and laughter, or else with sudden shouts. My cousins had frequent and fierce arguments with each other and, much to my surprise, with their parents as well. It was unimaginable that my brothers and I would ever yell at our parents — even looking as if you thought you might talk back was unthinkable. But my city cousins were in many ways unlike the people I had known. They were worldly-wise and sure of themselves. They spoke not only fast but peppered their speech with unusual slang. They suffered our presence with impatience one minute, ignored us the next. It seemed fitting that this topsy-turvy house should serve as my introduction to the North, where eventually all that I thought I knew about the world would be turned on its head. Even Durham, I would learn, was not exactly the place it had seemed to me.

My education began quickly, one evening shortly after we'd arrived. At dinner, someone mentioned the battles to desegregate the schools in the South. "Those children are having a terrible time," my uncle said, dipping his bread in his plate.

"But segregation is terrible too," my father said. "It's ridiculous. That we should be bused across town just to keep us from sitting next to a white child."

I listened intently. I was from the South, after all. The South had segregated schools. I knew the meaning of the word, since I had asked about it when I'd seen articles in the paper. Blacks kept separate from whites. How was it that my school had not been segregated?

"I didn't go to a segregated school," I offered.

"What are you talking about?" someone scoffed. "Of course you did."

"But that means with no white people," I maintained. Surely on this point I was right.

"And what white people do you think you know?" Uncle Eddie laughingly asked.

I opened my mouth and then closed it in a hurry. It was as if someone had abruptly switched on the lights in the middle of the night. I struggled to adjust my eyes to the brightness. I did not and would never confess what it was I had thought. It was too childish, too foolish, too humiliating. How could I have been so confused for so long? How people would laugh and tease me if they knew. So, I suddenly realized, my mother was not white, as I had long thought, nor was my aunt Julia, nor Jane Johnson, and certainly not my aunt Ginn. But if these people weren't, who were? I thought I had figured it out, and now I would have to start all over again. If white wasn't skin color, what was it?

"I'm going in to register Gwen and Garrett next week for school," my father said.

Uncle Eddie turned to me. "Are you ready to show those little white smarties what you're made of?" he asked. I hesitantly nodded my head.

That was all the preparation I remember. That I would be going to school with children the likes of which I had never met before. That I should show them something. And that it was important to my father that I be able to attend school where I pleased.

The registration did not go as smoothly as my parents had expected. My father went to the school alone, and came back in a dark mood. He reported that the principal had suggested that both my older brother and I be put back a grade. "We find that it helps the Southern Negro students to catch up," the principal had said.

"I told him to look at these report cards," my father said, pulling them out of his breast pocket. "I told him they don't need to do any catching up."

"I'm sure they had good grades," the principal had said, looking only cursorily at the cards. "But the standards here in the North are not the same as those you had in the South."

"If they can't keep up, then you can put them back," my father had said to him. "But you are not putting either of them back a grade. I want them in with the class they're supposed to be in. And I want them both put in with the brightest kids. If they can't keep up, then you call us."

My father was pacing around the kitchen. He was angry, and so was my mother. It was rare to see them both mad about the same thing. "Talk about putting somebody's children back. I wish I'd see the day they think they're going to put my children back!" He slammed one cabinet shut and then another. My father rarely got this way, but when he did, it was a frightful and fearsome sight. Something roiled out of him at those times, like dark blood from a deep wound. The principal was lucky: it sounded as if my father had restrained himself in a way that he didn't always restrain himself when he was mad. "Those children have had nothing but good report cards," my mother said, opening up the cards and looking them over. "And he's talking about keeping somebody back."

"You know how they are, what they think," my aunt Ginn said.

I wasn't supposed to be listening, but I sat very still in the corner of the room, proud of the way my father had stood up to that man, stood up for me and my brother. At the same time, the anger that all of them seemed to be sharing disturbed me. What did it mean? Whatever the principal had let loose, it now seemed to encompass so much more than him. I had always connected my parents' anger to something personal — something I or my brothers had done, or something that made them mad at each other. This anger was different. It crashed about the room, free-floating, huge, with a target that I couldn't see. And it didn't dissipate, but seemed to gather momentum as the evening went on. By the time my uncle Eddie came home, the tale had been retold a dozen times, and he too joined in the anger. It felt to me like an anger that was decades, maybe a lifetime, old.

When school began I was a little nervous, but mainly excited. The arguments about what grade and section in which I should be placed had faded from my memory, and after a summer of exploring the neighborhood and the novelty of living with a houseful of cousins, I was eager to meet my new teachers and classmates. I had even somewhat forgotten about white students. I knew they would be there, but since I still didn't know who or what they were, they too had faded from my mind. I was escorted to the classroom by a woman whose function wasn't explained and who seemed uninterested in me. "This is Gwen Parker, one of your new classmates," she told the class and the teacher.

The teacher — I guessed she was a white woman from her very pale skin and wavy hair, though I wasn't sure — barely looked up at me. "Take your seat when the bell rings," she said, and then went back to reading something on her desk. The rest of the class regarded me with a bit more interest, and I followed the lead of the others who were milling about the classroom and began to wander as well. I started with the shelves over by the window, where work and projects of one sort or another were on display, I guessed from the previous year, and I made my way slowly around the rim of the room. When I got to the back, I spied the bookshelves there and on the far side, and I ran to the books as if they were old friends. At least this was something that was known and trusted. I saw one book I recognized, by Dr. Seuss, and though I had outgrown him, much preferring the Bobbsey Twins now, the sight of the book filled me with a great rush of warmth. I snatched it up and began perusing the cover, and as fast as I had taken it, a girl appeared in front of me, the first white student with whom I had a face-to-face encounter.

She was a skinny, skittish girl with lank brown hair, and though I had noticed her when I first came into the classroom, I had not felt drawn to her in any way. I had noticed a shy girl with a pleasingly round face and blond hair who had smiled at me, and a brown-skinned girl about my color, with a very pretty face and perfectly done braids accented with bows. I had even noticed a group of scuffed-up-looking boys, in a variety of shades, whom I thought it might be best to steer clear of, but none of them approached me first.

"Dr. Seuss, he's my favorite," the girl with the damp brown hair said. Then she took the book from my hand. She didn't ask me for it, as I might have expected, but simply removed it from my less than firm grasp. As she did, she noticed the scar on my left hand, a pale creamy mark that was all that remained of a bad burn I'd gotten when I collided with a hot iron.

"Look at that," the girl said, pointing to my scar and at the same time grabbing my hand as she put the book down. She held it to examine it closer. "Right there," she said, staring intently. "Right there you're almost the same color as me." She thought for a second and then released my hand. "If you had a scar like that all over your body, why, then you could be white," she said.

She looked at me almost benevolently, as though she expected a thank-you for her suggestion. It was as if she had solved a problem that I wasn't even aware I had.

I looked at this girl and briefly thought her insane. What kind of lunatic must she be to make such a horrible suggestion, and in such a tone of voice. I wondered if this was the secret about white people that had been withheld from me all these years — that they were all crazy. I pulled away from her and moved to the front of the room, as far away from her as I could get. But her words wouldn't leave my mind. *You could be white, you could be white, you could be white.*

Once I was away from her, I reviewed in my mind what had happened. How odd that she had just snatched the book from my hand, and how familiar it was for her to touch me when we had not yet even exchanged names. It was as if she felt she had rights to me that I knew I had not given to her. And I also pondered her words — that being white would be something she was sure I would desire. The whole notion of whiteness was still a neutral concept to me, neither desired nor detested. What did being white mean to her?

As it turned out, the white students were not the only mystery to me at my new school. A group of Negro kids (we were not to say "colored" anymore) seemed to dislike me right from the start. There had been students with whom I hadn't been friends at my old school, but by and large I was well liked and friendly with all. I was not teased or picked on, and if someone was angry with me, it was because of something particular I'd done. Here, however, for the first time there seemed to be something about me that people didn't like that I couldn't begin to fathom. These students were not in my class, and I encountered them mainly on the playground or walking home from school.

"Little Miss Stuck-Up, Miss Smartypants," a girl said to me one day just outside school, pushing me as I tried to walk by. "Thinks she's better than everyone else," another girl echoed. "Well, she's not."

At first I wasn't sure they were talking to me. "Hey, you pushed me, watch where you're going," I said, and suddenly, there were three or four girls forming a ring around me.

"You want to make something of it, Miss Smartypants? Miss Skinny Ugly Girl with No Butt!"

I stood quietly and didn't move. I knew enough about fights to know that this was how they began, with somebody up in somebody's face, slinging words back and forth until finally the words erupted into a blow.

"No," I said cautiously, and the girls laughed derisively.

"Noooooo," they mocked back. "Listen to how she talks. Got that snooty voice and all."

Somebody pushed me again, just a little, and I took a step back.

"Didn't you hear what Cynthia said?" one of them taunted, pushing Cynthia, I guessed it was, forward. "She said your mama's a whore. You gonna let her say that 'bout your mama?"

Without even meaning to, I took a sharp intake of air. Nobody I knew talked this way, certainly not any children.

"She doesn't even know my mother," I replied. This seemed to egg them on, though I hadn't intended it. I'd meant it literally. I had never seen this girl, so how could she possibly know my mother? Besides, I wasn't sure what a whore was. It was a bad word, that much I knew, but I was pretty certain it was not true about my mother.

"She say you don't even know her mama, Cynthia," one of the girls said, pushing Cynthia so hard she collided with me. "You gonna take that?"

Cynthia, now close to me, looked me up and down with a sneer on her face. Perhaps I looked pitiful to her, or ridiculous. Or maybe her mood had shifted and whatever had initially made her angry had drifted away. But at least for the time being, she seemed to have lost her taste for this fight.

"She a dumb butt," Cynthia pronounced, as if I weren't worthy of her time. The other girls, following her lead, drifted away.

I didn't tell anyone at home what had happened, hoping it would never happen again. But it did, again and again. During a softball game on the playground, one of these same girls tripped me as I ran for home from third base. In the hallway, when we were changing from homeroom, another girl whispered something that sounded nasty about me as I passed. Finally, swearing him to secrecy, I asked my cousin Eddie what it was I had done. He said the problem was probably the way I talked.

"But I don't have a Southern accent anymore," I wailed, the tears I had held back springing forth at last.

Eddie explained. Not Southern, but kind of dicty. Proper. Stuck-up. "They probably think you're trying to act white or something," he told me.

This seemed like a cruel joke — that I should be accused of trying to act white when I had never, until this year, for the first time in my life, been in the same room with whites. But gradually, oh so slowly, I began to see that the things that had bound all of the black/colored/Negro people I had grown up with in Durham didn't apply in the same way here. What to me (if I'd been able to put it into words) was a big part of being colored — namely, having pride in yourself, working incredibly hard, always doing your best, and not using any excuse but yourself — was now somehow white and proper. Never mind that for me people had never been divided between rich and poor, smart and dumb, before: Mrs. Green, who cleaned people's houses for a living, and Lucille, who kept house for my grandmother, were as hard on their children about school and education as my parents were. Of course, in Durham, we had all gone to the same school, been in the same class, but here, as I later learned, I was in the advanced class, and the kids who were always threatening to beat me up were in what was known as the slow class. At the time, however, I didn't know any of that. I knew only that the skin color that had always meant safety and family and home to me was now a source of fear. And where being smart and getting good grades had been a matter of pride, I now was learning that these were things that someone else could hate about me.

I developed several strategies to avoid getting beaten up. The first was simple evasion. I would steer clear of those girls as much as I could, slowing down if I saw a group of them up ahead, giving them a wide berth on the playground, trying to hurry my exit from school so that I would not run into any of them. My refusal to fight went a long way. There was a choreography to a fight, a call and response that was preliminary of the event. Girls had to work themselves up to scratching and kicking and biting, and my refusal to trade insults and shoves kept me out of fights time and again. I even took a perverse pride in how I managed to escape with my skin intact. Gradually, however, in these encounters I began to feel exactly what these girls had initially accused me of. I started to act stuck-up and cocky, convinced that I was better than they. I amused myself by using words and sentences I thought they wouldn't understand. I became verbose and overly logical. I was by now disdainful of them, disdainful of their disregard for learning, disdainful of their broken language, disdainful of the way they cursed and the way they carried themselves.

"Your mother's a fucking whore," someone said my second year in the school.

"Well, if she's a whore, she obviously has intercourse, so that's a bit redundant, wouldn't you say?" I retorted. My little coterie of eggheads on the sidelines tittered.

One day an exchange like that ended with one of the girls challenging me in a different way.

"You think I'm stupid, don't you," she said. "Using all your big words, like I don't know what you're saying. You really think I'm stupid."

I looked at her. She was taller than I was by a good foot, and at least twice my girth. She was right in my face, and I noticed a large scar on her cheek. Her mouth was large and in motion, vigorously smacking on a wad of gum. "Yes," I said, looking her straight in the eye, a surge of anger rushing through me. "Yes, I think you're stupid."

For just a second it felt good. I felt triumphant and big. I saw her face and the look that flitted across it. I saw I had at last struck a nerve. Why, she believed herself stupid, I realized; it was what she genuinely felt. In fact, the fleeting look on her face told me volumes about her — that being stupid was both her greatest fear and her safest refuge, and the word itself had an echo so huge that just the sound of it cast out any other sense she might have had of herself. It was the sum and total of what she thought and had been told about herself. And it was what I had been accused of thinking all along, and now finally I'd said it.

I saw the look in her eyes and still I savored the moment. I was glad that I'd said it, glad that I had really struck back — not just protected myself, but hurt back as I had been hurt. The other girls hooted and brayed. I was going to get it now. *Fight, fight, fight,* they all began screaming, pushing the big girl closer to me.

I knew this time I had gone too far. The look of pain on the girl's face had disappeared, and now there was a look of pure fury. I was suddenly, desperately afraid. I wished fervently that I could grab those words out of the air and stuff them back into my mouth. She was going to hurt me if it was the last thing she did, hurt me as I had just hurt her. It was personal now.

My hands and knees began to shake and I tried to just walk on and ignore the jostling. I hoped no one could see me trembling or hear the loud thuds my heart was making against the walls of my chest. I walked faster and they walked faster. I didn't say anything else — I couldn't if I tried, my mouth was that dry — and every few yards someone would shove me again, yelling *fight, fight, fight*. After each shove, the big girl would circle in front of me menacingly.

"You think you're so smart, don't you, you little shit. Well, you better have another think coming. Calling me stupid. I'm going to show you who's stupid."

Miraculously, with this slow, circling minuet, we made it nearly to my house without anything happening. I was only one last, long block away. A few girls had tired of the spectacle and turned off to go their own way home. But the big girl and two of her best friends remained. The big girl confronted me one last time. "I ain't stupid," she said. "You gonna be sorry you ever said that."

I was no longer as mad as I'd been when I hurled that word at her. I was even, in a small way, beginning to move beyond fear. I looked at my adversary again. I realized that I didn't know if she was stupid or not. I didn't know her at all, just as she didn't know me. It suddenly seemed so ridiculous, this tug of war we were caught in, neither of us able to escape the sides to which we'd been assigned. I saw too that I had run out of options. She was going to beat me up today, whether I fought back or not. That I felt I didn't deserve it, that I had never thought ill of her until she had driven me to it, didn't matter. Here we were, and here we were going to be, until one of us was in tears and perhaps bleeding.

I recalled fights I had seen on TV westerns, where someone wound up his arm and threw his weight behind it. So I did as I'd seen the cowboys do, and to add the advantage of surprise, I threw the first blow. First to her stomach, where I thought she wouldn't expect it, and then to her face, not a slap but a punch. She reeled backward a little, stunned, and then I took both of my hands and threw my whole weight against her, stretching up to push at the center of her chest. With all I had in me I pushed. And much to my amazement she went down. It was almost easy. She grunted when I punched her and then she was down. And then I ran for all I was worth. I had only that one long block to go and it was all downhill. I cut through yards, careened around the corner closest to my house. I didn't waste a second looking back. I don't know if they chased me at all. I do know I made it home safely, and I swore to myself that, having escaped with my face intact, I would never give in to my anger like that again. That night, when my breathing had finally returned to normal, I recalled the look on the big girl's face. It was a look I would later recognize when I taught briefly as a substitute teacher — a look of the left-behind, the discarded. I saw the girl's eyes opening as I said the word "stupid," and behind them I felt a wide and deep sorrow. In my fear, I hadn't been able to feel it, but I felt it now and was ashamed that I'd been the cause of such pain. I promised my secret gods that I would never call anyone stupid again.

With time, I gave up on the idea that any of these girls would ever be my friends. I began to push them out of my mind. They grew tired of taunting me, and even the big girl was not particularly eager to gain her revenge. I settled instead on making friends in my own class. It was my literal class at school, but looking back, it might as well have been posted as my social class too. If all of us were not as bright as the brightest in the class, we all shared a background of parents who not only believed in the value of a good education, but who had, as my parents did, the wherewithal and the self-confidence to fight for it if need be.

For all of my elementary and junior high schooling in

Mount Vernon, I was with the same group of students. Having been separated into sections according to promise and ability in the fourth grade, we remained that way through junior high. Kids occasionally transferred when their families moved into and out of the area, but I don't remember anyone leaving the group where they'd started. There were about six or seven Negroes in my class, three girls and three or four boys. All of our parents were college-educated, and most had degrees beyond college. There was Chris Hall, quiet and studious, whose mother was a counselor and whose stepfather was a businessman. Chris went on to become an engineer at one of the subsidiaries of AT&T. There was Virginius Bragg, tall and good looking, with a Southern drawl and a leisurely Southern manner that he refused to lose. There was DeVerges Jones, tall and impossibly skinny, whose mother and mine were close friends. Among the girls was Nora Davis — daughter of the actors Ossie Davis and Ruby Dee — and Michele, who had been the pretty girl with the bows. Michele got a figure before any of us, and she seemed to know how to straddle the cultural line between the Negro kids in our class and those in the rest of our school. Nora and I were the only two girls out of the fifty or so graduating from the sixth grade into junior high whose parents had insisted we wear socks and patent-leather flats, not stockings and heels like the other girls. Nora and I were friends for a while — she and her family lived around the corner from the first house we lived in after staying with Aunt Ginn — but she was often traveling with her parents. Michele, though we liked each other, seemed to be way out of my league in both looks and cool. I didn't know the first thing about cool, and I was Southern to boot, hopelessly backward and geeky. I was also friends with DeVerges — he and I occasionally went to parties at Jack and Jill, a social club for middle-class blacks. At those parties I was often shunned by the other girls and boys because I was brown, not light-skinned, and because I did not have naturally wavy or straight, so-called "good" hair. Sometimes a small group of us from school, blacks and whites, had parties in each other's basements.

I did begin to make friends with white girls too — slowly, and again always girls in my class. Whenever I stopped to wonder where "white" fit into the definition of these new friendships, I found that it had not gained a foothold. It was still a largely formless concept to me. From bits and pieces, I was constructing the meaning of race I would one day understand, but for many long years I took each element in isolation and tried to fit it into a scheme that I knew. So it never occurred to me then that the white girl I walked to school with every day might not have played with me after school because I was black, that she might have rushed me out of the house to keep her father from seeing me, that she might have had a whole category for me that I did not have for her. I can never know for sure. And as it turned out, my best friend was also a white girl.

Cecilia lived up the street from the house my parents bought the second year we were in the North. Cecilia and I were as alike temperamentally as we were dissimilar physically. She was round and firm where I was tall and bony. Her blond hair, when she brushed it, followed the brush into the air and caught the sunlight; my brown legs wound and unwound like the branches of a sapling as I turned in a chair in her kitchen. She was pink-skinned all year and I was the color of a hazelnut in the winter, tanned to coconut brown in summer. But we were the two top students in our class through most of elementary and junior high school, both alert and curious, dogged in our quest for good grades. And we both got them. But it took me a while to notice a puzzling difference in our teachers' responses to my performance. Returning a test, a teacher might say to Cecilia, "Good job," and maybe give her a little pat on the shoulder. My equally good score would go without comment. I would eagerly raise my hand to answer a question, but rarely would the teacher call on me. If I persisted — "Miss So-and-so," I would call out, "I have the answer" — a correct response was never greeted with a smile of approval.

I explained all this to myself in personal terms. The teachers knew Cecilia better, or I was unintentionally doing something they didn't like. It simply did not occur to me for a long time that the reason I was so often ignored might have something to do with the color of my skin. It took a dramatic incident to bring the fact home to me. It came with a rare creative-writing assignment from our English teacher, Mr. Bollen. I had had many chances to show off my love of words in essays and on tests, but this was the first time in my new school I had been told to write a poem. For me, writing poetry had always been a secret pleasure. I had been writing poems for years, my first a few words on a napkin when I was five. I was so excited about the assignment I could hardly wait to get home and begin. I worked hard on my poem from the day it was assigned until the night before it was due. I was proud of the result. The poem rhymed in all the right places. I had struggled to make it about something on the surface and about something below the surface as well, with the two connected. *A little girl is wandering in the night,* it began. *Her heart is filled with fear. And she is walking filled with fright, for danger may be near.*

I waited impatiently for Mr. Bollen to read and grade our papers. Finally the day arrived. He called out each of our names. When I heard mine, I nearly skipped up to the desk to get my paper. Cecilia had already gotten hers and smiled at me as she returned to her seat, to let me know that she was pleased with her grade. The teacher handed me my poem, and as I walked back to my seat I looked down and saw my grade. I was sure I was not reading it correctly. I sat down, put the paper on my desk, checked that I did not have it upside down or sideways, and read my grade again. C-minus. It was a bold red letter at the top of the paper. C-minus. Almost a D. I had never received a grade lower than a B-plus. C-minus to me was as bad as an F. It said failure, poor quality, unworthy. I could hardly wait for the class to be over. I rushed to the teacher's desk.

"Mr. Bollen," I began, "this grade, this C —" I couldn't even finish the word. Tears sprang to my eyes. "This can't be right," I managed to say.

He looked at me coolly.

"The grade is correct," he said, without even checking either my paper or his record book.

All I managed was. "Why?" I knew if I tried to talk more I would dissolve into the hiccupping tears that I hated so much.

He stared at me as if he regretted my birth. It was a look filled with contempt, and with anger. "There is no way you could have written that poem," he said. "I searched all weekend, looking for where you might have copied it from."

I imagined him, just for a second, at home. My mother was a teacher, I knew that teachers ate food, drove cars, fell asleep on the sofa with their mouths open, snoring. I tried to picture Mr. Bollen in a small apartment with not enough light. With an undershirt on rather than a white shirt and a tie. Hunched over an open book of poetry.

"If I'd been able to find where you plagiarized it from," he went on, "I would have given you an F. But since I couldn't find it, you are lucky I gave you the C-minus."

After wanting it for so long, I had Mr. Bollen's undivided attention. He'd spent an entire weekend on me, all to prove I was a fake. I looked down at my feet to see if they were still on the floor. I felt sure that someone had hit me, that I must have gone down. But no, my feet were below me, my hands still outstretched, my paper in hand. Right in front of him, the paper was starting to shake. I knew that if I spoke, the words might come out as a squeal, but I had to speak. I would make him understand that I wasn't a cheater. I would change his scornful look.

"But I wrote it, Mr. Bollen, I wrote it," I said. "I didn't copy it. I would never. I made it up out of my head, just like you told us to."

He looked at me again, with an expression so disdainful that it made me mute and invisible and impossibly small.

Then he turned away from me, and I took my paper and fled. I don't remember where I ran. Just my feet carrying me, away. I didn't want anyone to see me. I didn't want anyone's eyes on me. His cold regard had sent an awful message: You are a cheater, a fraud. Dirty, sneaky, low. And something worse even, something so despicable that I couldn't even name it. It was crawling all over me, dripping down to the floor. Everywhere I turned, there it was, this something about me that made Mr. Bollen look at me that way.

Days passed before I knew what that thing was. Days of

wondering what it was about me that could be so unworthy. Days of horrible rawness. My parents cursed when I told them. They knew what it was, they disparaged Mr. Bollen, and even though I heard what they said, still I didn't know. I agonized for days, sifting through all that I'd experienced. And then suddenly the mud sank to the bottom and the water ran clear.

Mr. Bollen was certain that I couldn't have written that poem because it was too good, and a Negro couldn't possibly write that well. He looked at me as he looked at all Negro children — when he was forced to look at them at all. My teachers didn't call on me because they didn't expect me to have the answers, and when they learned that I did, they ignored me as much as they could because they didn't want me to have them. They didn't congratulate me for the high marks I got on my tests because a Negro's good grades were not an occasion for joy. They didn't pat me on the shoulder as they did with Cecilia because they didn't want to touch me.

It all came together: my parents' bitter anger, the things that I heard them saying about some of my teachers, Mr. Bollen's comments, the girl who had taken my book that first day. In this grade school picture book, Negroes were loud and stupid and didn't get good grades in school and were dirty and sneaky and lied and cheated and were everything and anything that was bad and filthy and low. Not all of my teachers believed all of these things — some of them thought none of these thoughts — but many of them shared at least some of those views. So I learned that my math teacher told another teacher that the reason I did so well in math was that my mother, who was also a math teacher, spent nights tutoring me and doing my homework on the side. Another teacher, I learned, had asked Cecilia if I copied her homework. Another had asked her to sit apart from me when we took tests, so that I wouldn't be able to cheat, as they were convinced I had been doing all along.

I returned to school with this new knowledge, and after my initial hurt lost some of its tenderness, sought its confirmation. I looked for the reluctant hand that wouldn't touch mine when it handed back a paper. I looked for the averted eyes, the smug grimace when I blurted out the right answer. I was a detective, and once I'd gathered up my observations, I was the judge and jury as well. Guilty, I decided. Guilty, guilty, not guilty. I had another purpose now, another way of doing things, another motivation to drive me.

I would show them. I would rub their faces in it. They had never met a Negro who was smart? Well, they were meeting one now. I wouldn't just get the scores and the grades, I would lord it over them. I used the thesaurus when I wrote my papers, searching for words that even the teachers wouldn't know. I corrected their math and spelling errors as they wrote on the board. I argued with them now over test questions, not to get another point, but to show them they were wrong. If one of us had to be stupid, I was determined that it would not be I. I remembered my grandmother Parker's words, that there was nothing that beat being smart, especially if you were colored, since it was the last thing white people expected.

If the North was to me a new world that was decidedly unpleasant, it was also, as my father had originally promised, a new world of dazzling possibility. My first real introduction to all that lay beyond the red dirt of North Carolina was New York, a city that did not merely dazzle but made me feel like a coconspirator in its splendor. See what the two of us can be, it seemed to whisper, see how much more there is to see and know. My mother and father took us on day-long excursions, riding the Circle Line, going up to the top of the Empire State Building, out to the Statue of Liberty, to the Guggenheim, to the Museum of Modern Art, to the Met. Each year we went to the Radio City Christmas and Easter shows, standing on line for hours for tickets, the camaraderie and adventure of keeping warm on the line as much fun as the show. We went shopping and window-shopping all up and down Fifth Avenue, in stores like Saks and Lord & Taylor and B. Altman, where others of our complexion were nearly as rare as mannequins that talked. My mother had a system for navigating the salesladies — who would either ignore us or hover too closely, as if they feared we might steal — and that was to know exactly what she wanted and to avoid or ignore *them* until she was ready to pay. I was too taken with it all, however, to pay that much mind. I darted in and out of the clothes racks, peered down the side of the escalators, walked a few paces behind my mother so I could watch myself multiplying in the banks of mirrors that cascaded on either side of us.

In the North, we also traveled. We had often gone away in the summers in North Carolina, but we rarely went farther than Virginia. Now we went on long car trips to see the rest of the country. We went to Chicago and visited the Museum of Science and Industry one summer, to Detroit to see the Greenfield Village and the Henry Ford Museum another summer, to Boston to walk the Freedom Trail. When my brother Garrett got older, we even went on a tour of Ivy League schools, so that when the time came for choosing a college, neither my brother nor I would have to do it sight unseen. On our trips, we stayed in hotels and pored over guidebooks. We rode trains and buses and streetcars and trolleys, and went out to both family-style and fancy restaurants. While my mother always tried to steer us toward the cheaper choices on the menu, my father would tell us we could have anything we wanted. His attitude was worth more than the lobster or shrimp I invariably chose. It kicked open the doors of the world and held them wide for us. If people stared at us in the hotels and restaurants and trolley cars and tour buses and museums, we were too busy to notice.

My father was clearly hungry for the world, and his hunger affected us all. Whenever we awoke on a trip, it would be to the sight of my father returning from somewhere: even at 7 A.M. he would have already gone out, seen something, learned something new. He would have read over all the guidebooks and mapped out the day. Come on, come on, he would urge, the day is slipping by, there's so much in this city to see and do.

Wherever we went, my father would strike up conversations with strangers. I did not find it remarkable then, but I find it remarkable now: he was totally unafraid of the world, believed himself equal to any man or woman, and most astoundingly, he approached the world without rancor or bitterness. He could become angry, did become angry, when he encountered prejudice, but usually his anger was short-lived and did not sully the next encounter. If someone was willing to meet him halfway, he would willingly take the first several steps. His was an infectious and buoyant spirit, offering us a great lesson in how to navigate the world, particularly a world that at times was less than hospitable. Perhaps most surprising of all for a Southern man — reared on Jim Crow, his own ambitions and sights narrowed by the choices that had been open to him, his experiences with whites in the South often decidedly unpleasant — he did not see only color when he looked at a person. Oh, he noted it, knew it. But riding a train he would strike up a conversation with the midwestern farmer and his wife on holiday with their three children, and later he would come back to our seats and tell us of the long hours that farm life demanded, the machinery the farmer was trying to buy, the distances the children traveled by bus to school. He could strip away in an instant what should have, might have, divided him from others. And if he found differences, he found them interesting, telling. Life for him was variety and change, and my father was eager to see and to know. He leapt barriers as if they did not exist, and watching him, taking our cue from him, we leapt them as well.

Looking back, I can only imagine how determined my father was that his children should have the whole world in full measure, that whatever other people knew and were exposed to, we should know and be exposed to as well. He girded us with facts and figures and experiences as if they were armor. This museum was designed by Frank Lloyd Wright, he'd tell us. It was finished in 1959. Its continuous circular walkway was one of the first of its kind. These paintings are by Rubens and Van Dyck. They are part of the Baroque period. These are by Vermeer and Van Gogh. Henry Ford built four different cars before he made the Model T. Science, art, history, music, theater, food — we would have it all. Even as he went casually into debt to finance these excursions, he had his rationales. "I don't want them to grow up thinking lobster is a big deal," he would tell my mother.

This was one source of constant friction between my parents: what sort of accommodation the world would demand. In Durham, I had never thought of my mother as shy or diffident, but the North brought out a different side of her, a side that was more easily cowed. I was always taken aback by this, because to me, to all of us, my mother was a huge figure: she brooked no dissent from any of her children, and if need be, she could lift the roof off the house with her anger. But outside the house, among strangers, particularly among white people she did not know, she could turn reticent and cautious.

"I don't think they're serving yet," my mother would say, turning from the entryway of a restaurant she feared might be too expensive or less than welcoming.

"I'll go find the maitre d'," would be my father's response. On spying him, my father would call out confidently, "Table for five." It was my mother who noticed the stares that might accompany us on one of our forays. My father would just laugh and say, "Well, what can they do?"

There lay their differences in a nutshell: all my father needed was access, and the rest he would get on his own; my mother hoped that the world would welcome her, and when it didn't, she retracted her feelings behind an imposing façade of "proper" colored reserve. People in Durham had always said how much I was like my father; in the North I learned I was my mother's daughter as well. I might stride in, apparently eager and confident like my father, but like my mother, as the years went by, I grew alert to the lingering stare that dampened my own hopes for acceptance.

Though I had found places here in the North where I felt welcome and safe, for the most part they were private ones. Public spaces I had to negotiate, I had to be wary of, and nowhere was this more true than at school. School was where I consistently encountered the world; it was my neighborhood, my mini-community. As a Negro child, the lesson that the North persistently taught me was that the community at large was not interested in extending its reach to encompass people like me.

A news survey in April 1960 had revealed that, despite the *Brown vs. Board of Education* Supreme Court decision six years earlier outlawing separate-but-equal schools, 94 percent of the South's Negro students still attended segregated schools. Though many had thought the problem was confined to the South, assessments of schools in most parts of the North revealed similar divisions. In fact, in the fall of the same year, eight Negro parents had been arrested in a town next to Mount Vernon for a sit-in protesting the de facto segregation at one of the town's all-white elementary schools. There were similar protests, sit-ins, and boycotts all across the country. It was the time, in short, when Negro parents were pushing their children forward into the white world, attempting to claim a space for them.

By the time I was fourteen, in 1964, my parents had bullied me into whatever accelerated classes our neighborhood school, Graham School, had to offer. The teachers and administrators had for the most part given up the fight to keep me out, had in fact made of our small, quarrelsome, determined middle-class Negro group an exception to the general rule that the blacks should be placed in classes outside the college-prep track. (Though even at the high school level, they would keep trying. My older brother was told by a school counselor that he shouldn't bother applying to an Ivy League school, that it was far above what he could expect to achieve.) Beyond our group, the school I attended on the south side of town was structured so that it was almost two separate schools: one for the college-bound students and one for the rest. Meanwhile, the housing patterns of the city had crystallized to such a degree that there were, in effect, two Mount Vernons: a mostly white and upper-middle-class Mount Vernon north of the railroad tracks, and a soon to be largely black and increasingly poorer south side. Though the first black residents, like my family, had been middle class, most had been steered to the south side by real estate agents (as indeed our family had when we looked for a house), and they had been followed, in the intervening years, by the working-class and poorer blacks who were fleeing the city. These too were concentrated on the south side. With a relaxing of zoning and housing requirements, by 1964 there were pockets of housing projects and single-occupancy rooming houses grouped on the south side. As a result, this area began to experience some of the problems reminiscent of the metropolitan area from which many of the residents had fled.

The schools reflected this change. The racial composition of the north side schools was overwhelmingly white, as high as 96 or 97 percent in some schools. The racial population of the south side schools was overwhelmingly minority — mainly black, over 90 percent at one school. Although the school I attended was nearly 50 percent minority, predominantly black, segregation within the school meant that in my classes, the proportions of blacks were far lower. So in a city with a minority population of about 20 percent, and where nearly 45 percent of the elementary school population was nonwhite, many of the schools were overwhelmingly composed of only blacks or only whites.

The move to change this de facto segregation of the Mount Vernon schools was initiated by several events. The first was a lawsuit in the neighboring town of New Rochelle in which the court had found that claimants were entitled to relief where it could be shown that there had been past discrimination in the drawing of school boundaries, or that the appropriate officials had ignored racial imbalance in the drawing of such boundaries. A second impetus was the request by New York State's commissioner of education to the Mount Vernon Board of Education that it report to the state the situation regarding racial imbalance in its schools and propose a plan of action to address the problem. A third was simply the tenor of the times, as more and more states and localities were grappling with the issue of segregation in the nation's schools.

Perhaps seeking to avoid a compulsory solution from above, Mount Vernon took, from the start, the principled high road. The school board presented a laudatory statement of policy: it would correct forthwith whatever imbalances existed. It appointed a twelve-member Citizens' Advisory Committee on racial imbalance. It also hired an outside expert, Dr. Dan Dodson of the Center for Human Relations and Community Studies at New York University, to assess the situation and provide the school board with a plan of action.

I learned about the issue as I learned about most such issues — at home, by overhearing conversations between my parents. What struck me first about these discussions was the vast gulf between my mother and my father in their take on things. It was a gulf I had been noticing more and more, but it was particularly wide on this issue. With this move to the North, I had learned that my father was essentially an optimist on human nature, and as a result, he and my mother differed profoundly over the kind of treatment they expected from the world.

As I listened to their arguments about desegregation, I realized I was caught in the middle. My father thought that the North would be different; he relied on rationality and reason. My mother, however, as a teacher in the junior high, was at the schools every day. She met with parents of the children she taught and overheard the teachers in the teachers' lounge as they spoke disparagingly of the south side schools and the children who attended them. Like my father, I too found it hard to believe, even when the facts stared me in the face, that people could reject others on the basis of something as ridiculous as the color of their skin. Yet like my mother, I knew firsthand the cold indifference with which many teachers regarded me.

At bottom, the optimist in me won. I was carried away by the high-minded statements the school board members made in the press, by the reasonableness with which people comported themselves when they were interviewed for the numerous articles that appeared in the paper. This was not the Deep South with its fire hoses and snarling police dogs, where white parents vowed they would die before allowing their children to be sullied by being forced to commingle with blacks. Here the future was a matter of rational discussion among caring experts, adults, parents, who it seemed to me would carry the day.

Dodson was the first to contribute his opinion, and it came out strongly in favor of a busing plan to integrate the schools. Mount Vernon, according to Dodson's report, had a chance to turn away from the past and relentlessly face the future, to seize the day and create a true community, one based not on narrow neighborhoods, but on shared citizenship and responsibility. The true neighborhood, argued the report, had to be larger than the few blocks around one's own house.

The Citizens' Advisory Committee found in favor of the Dodson report, with only one member dissenting. I felt buoyed when I read the paper each day, as more and more people seemed to weigh in on the side of the new plan. There were dissenting opinions on the editorial page, but they seemed to be in the minority, lingering prejudices that would recede with the advance of the newly dawning day.

Still, my mother was adamant and pessimistic. "You don't know these people like I do," she told my father. "If it goes against them, every one of them will move. That, or put their children in private school."

The school board's decision came a week after the public meeting to discuss the issue. The meeting was held at the high school, and even as people gathered in the parking lot, you could feel the tension. At the meeting itself, people lined up on each side of the auditorium, patiently waiting their turn at the microphone. People spoke for themselves, for their neighbors, for a friend. They all spoke quickly, as they were allotted only three minutes apiece. Some talked softly, and it was hard to hear them. Some shouted, as if they didn't trust the microphone to work. I tried to count for and against, but lost track because I was concentrating so hard on those who spoke against the proposal. I heard them explain how terrible it would be for children not to know the joy of playing in their own neighborhood with friends they had made in school, how dangerous it would be to put six- and seven-year-olds on a bus and make them ride all the way across town, how nice it was to have your children come home for lunch rather than eat at school. But what I really heard was what was under the words: I don't want my children sitting in a classroom with you, I don't want them to make friends with you, I don't want their arms to brush against yours in the hall. To me, whatever their actual numbers, these people seemed to make up the majority. They represented the larger world that I longed to be part of, but that did not want me to be one of its members.

The next day, the newspaper reported that the meeting had been orderly, the crowd had been respectful and well behaved. Clearly the reporter who covered the meeting hadn't seen the man who exchanged words with my mother as we were leaving and then spat at her and called her a nigger bitch. Still, the bulk of the meeting had been restrained and polite and I had hope. The paper said that the numbers had actually come out more in favor of the busing proposal than against it. Other citizens' groups voiced their opinions, urging Mount Vernon to do the right and righteous thing. I tried to cling to those words.

But in the end my mother was proved right. When the school board met the next week, it voted overwhelmingly to reject the busing plan. In fact, the busing plan was scarcely mentioned. Only two people dissented: Mary Ellen Cooper, the only black on the board, and one white man. Apparently, the people who were against the plan all along had been working quietly behind the scenes. I had been misled by the surface civility. The politeness was just the way it was done in the North. The disdain was just as deep and as real.

It was during this same year that my parents began discussing in earnest the idea of sending me away to high school — to a college preparatory school, a boarding school. A teacher friend of my mother's had told her about A Better Chance, a scholarship program for Negro students to attend such schools. It seemed to be designed for kids from the inner city, but the only criterion was race. My parents wanted to send me to a prep school because it would offer the kind of intellectual challenge the public school lacked. I was interested mainly because it meant getting away. Not away from home, but away from all that Mount Vernon had come to mean to me: away from those girls who glowered at me in the halls; away from feeling that I should apologize for studying; away from those Jack and Jill parties, the other end of the Negro spectrum, where I still didn't fit; and now away from decisions about race that so thoroughly depressed me.

The overwhelming sentiment of the community had been spoken, and it was against people like me. The whites on the north side of town would not be forced to flee (though eventually they would, the racial problems mushrooming just as Dr. Dodson had predicted they would). They would simply keep the blacks penned in on the south side, and for as long as they could, they would ignore us. I wanted no more of a town that defined me as a problem, like a disease that was likely to spread.

As I sifted through the catalogues of the schools my parents and I were considering, I saw smiling girls walking arm in arm across huge expanses of green. That was almost as important to me as the smiles: the trees and the green. They reminded me of Durham. I could be happy in such a world, I thought, a world filled with students lolling on the grass, playing sports, their heads bent over books. At last I would be with students who studied hard and were not ashamed of that fact, who believed that getting good grades was a fine thing. These schools were not recoiling from the thought of someone like me attending; they were actively seeking me out. This I decided was the real North, the North my father had talked so much about, a place of real opportunity and harmony.

THREE

Bitsy, Muffy, and Me

THE DISTANCE from Mount Vernon to the Kent School in Connecticut, where I started school at the age of fifteen in the fall of 1965, was not far in miles. But though the drive couldn't have taken more than a few hours, it felt to me as if it stretched on through the better part of a day, as my past receded slowly behind me, bit by bit. My parents and I made our way over country roads through small towns with names reminiscent of England, where county and town both bore the same name. With each mile we traveled, all that was familiar to me was swallowed up by the bends in the road. Everything, it seemed, had narrowed down to this moment. I had said good-bye to my brothers, who had not come along on the trip. They were already escaping from me, back to a time marked Then, in that past when I still lived at home.

I spent the whole trip reaching backward in my mind for pieces of my life that were continually disappearing from view. Everything that arose bore the indelible stamp: the last time. I looked at my mother and father and thought, This is the last time I will sit with them in this car in this way. This is the last time my parents will turn and speak to me as they were doing right now, familiarly, without thought. From here on out, I will no longer be one of them, not in a day-to-day way. I will return to them only for brief sojourns, a visitor to my own home. It was as if I were suddenly in a boat that I had unwittingly, and now unwisely I feared, pushed away from the shore.

The school lay on the outskirts of the town of Kent, itself no more than a quarter of a mile from end to end: a drugstore, a Laundromat, a post office, a small grocery store. Rolling hills, farmland, and vintage colonial houses were Kent's claim to fame at that time, a quiet fame that only in later years gave way to seasonal art galleries and ice cream parlors, when Hollywood actors and investment bankers discovered its charms. The turnoff for the school was just before you entered the town, marked by a signpost: *Kent School, 1906.* We turned and went over a small bridge and the boys' school opened up on our left. The boys' school was the original campus, lying along the banks of the Housatonic River, where its crew team perfected the strokes that took it to the Henley regatta in England each year. The girls' school was a recent addition, built in 1960, four and a half miles up a winding country road, atop Skiff Mountain.

We finally arrived at the top of the mountain, and in front of each dorm we saw cars like ours, filled with trunks and blankets and record players and loose shoes, the occupants making their way to their rooms laden like small mules. Suddenly no one looked as friendly as they had in the catalogue. "Old girls" — the term for the returning students — called out in shrill voices as they spied their old friends, and they ran into each other's arms, leaving their families standing around, as mine did, looking momentarily bewildered, tired, a little taken aback by such enthusiasm. The old girls ignored both their parents and the rest of us, the new girls.

The dorms themselves were functional and unadorned, scrubbed clean at the end of each term by the students, with a common room at the center and the bedrooms and baths branching off hallways running from end to end. Each room had two beds, two desks and desk chairs, and two movable wardrobes. I later learned that the furniture could be arranged in endlessly creative ways to carve up the space, but I just left the furniture where it stood, piling my things on one bed against the wall, carefully unpacking my sweaters and skirts and blouses into the wardrobe. My room looked away from the school, out over the skating pond that lay behind it, and then off, in the far distance, to the road that had carried us here. I stole glances at it as my mother helped me unpack and my father brought the heavy things in. With little in the way of personal belongings allowed, it was all unpacked in no time.

I'm not exactly sure what I expected, but what I prayed for then was that my parents would declare this a terrible mistake and summarily bundle me back into the car, where we would all flee. But once I was unpacked, my parents exchanged greetings with my new roommate and her parents, and my father said it was growing late and there was a long drive ahead. We said our goodbyes. My father expressed his concern about the coming darkness and the less than familiar roads. Then they left, almost breezily it seemed, and it was only because I knew my father would never relent that I did not chase after them.

As I watched their car disappear over the horizon, I was suddenly overtaken by a wave of homesickness for which I could never have prepared. After all, I was fifteen — an age when I thought my parents were useless relics of a time gone by and my two brothers, my older brother Garrett and my younger brother Tony, surely were dispensable. But now that my parents were gone, I wanted desperately to be with them. I wanted my brothers to be there so I could fight with them for space in the car. I wanted to listen to my parents chat and bicker. I wanted to be with them as the afternoon turned into evening and as the evening turned into night. I saw them arriving home without me, perhaps stopping for something to eat along the way, and I ached with longing for the familiar sights and sounds of my family: for my mother's and father's snoring at night, for the gossip between my mother and aunts after school. Already, only fifteen or so minutes into this new life, I missed Tony's furious ten-year-old dignity, his resourcefulness as he gathered bottles to turn in for pennies in his wagon, his quirky gap-toothed smile. I missed Garrett's whispered phone conversations with, I suspected, a girlfriend. I missed his goofy jokes, his singing some song out of key. I even missed the noise and clutter that was part of our house, the smell of my mother's perfume, her coffee cup left on the kitchen counter, the hydrangeas and roses that bloomed in the yard.

More than anything, I wanted to be home again — not just home, but bosomed, defended and safe. Whatever I might have navigated before, I had not done it alone. My family had extended around me like an extra layer of skin, warm and protecting. Whatever was to come, and despite all of my earlier optimism and bravado, I would have to face it alone.

There was no time to linger at the window, however. Already it was time to go somewhere, my first official event: the headmaster's tea, to welcome the new girls. It was hosted by the headmaster and his wife, Syd and Nancy Towle. They lived at the center of the girls' school campus, in a big white house with black shutters, and attendance, like nearly every event at the school, wasn't optional.

I changed into the dress that was to be worn every Saturday and Sunday and on all special occasions, a simple blue A-line that the girls in the school called, appropriately enough, our Saturday night. It fell over my body as all dresses did — unimpeded, no hips or breasts to slow down its fall. And I thought again: What had possessed me? What had ever made me think I could do such a thing, leave my home and all I knew to come to this strange place for school, where I knew no one, where I would have to sleep in a room with a stranger, where I and one other girl were the first Negro girls ever admitted. I didn't want to be the first anything. I felt I was not an able representative of anything except the skinny and the gracelessly shy.

As I stood there listening to the sounds of other girls leaving the dorm, the dorm doors at the end of the hall opening and closing, just a little bit of cooler air skittering down the hall, I realized that this was only the beginning, that the world itself was going to keep coming, one thing after another, things for which I could never really prepare for, and it was going to be this way for the rest of my life.

I walked to the headmaster's house with my new roommate, a returning girl. Her name was Bobbie Gladding, and it fit: she was nice and friendly in a bouncy way. At the door, Bobbie started to introduce me to the headmaster's wife, but it seemed she already knew who I was. "Gwen Parker," she said. "Welcome to Kent School." She extended her hand. I took it and was surprised by how flaccid her grip was, as if she were in danger of slipping away. She looked weary to me, her smile as tired as her hand. How many times, I wondered, had she stood at this door, smiling this way? Just then Bobbie saw someone she knew and took off to a room to the left. The headmaster's wife immediately but subtly pointed me in the other direction. "Have some punch and cakes and sandwiches in here, dear," she said, walking me to a long room, a sun porch lined with plants. She waved toward a table at the back of the room, and I knew instantly that this was the room where the girls with problems were steered. Perhaps she thought she was being kind, but as I looked around, there was no mistaking the snap judgment she'd made. There we all stood, all manner of rejects: too tall, too short, unattractive, overweight. My own crimes I supposed were multiple: brown, shapeless, and far too tall.

Now I felt so self-conscious that I feared I was glowing. Surely even my thoughts were emblazoned in neon over my head. There was no one anywhere in sight who looked remotely like me. There was no one this brown, no one whose hair had been so harshly treated with chemicals — I'd gotten my first "relaxer" in preparation for coming to the school — no one who had ever been this tall or this awkward, whose feet were as big as mine. There was nowhere to move or to stand. I tried to swallow and my throat closed so tightly that I feared I might choke.

I thought I had stopped breathing, and felt that if I stayed rooted to that spot a moment longer I would probably topple to the floor. So I forced my feet to move in the direction of the table piled with food at the other end of the room. There was red punch, small crustless sandwiches, and tiny, perfectly frosted cakes, each the size of a thimble. I would not risk the punch — my hands felt too shaky for that — I wouldn't tackle the sandwiches that were stacked precariously high, but those tiny cakes lined up in neat rows seemed like a challenge I could handle. I would take one and one only, and eat it slowly. For those wonderful moments while eating, I would be engaged. My hands would have a function instead of hanging like meat cleavers at my side, and my mouth, unfit for words, could chew. As I reached the table, I thought, Good, I have acted.

I took up a cake, a pink one, and lifted it to my mouth for a bite. It was sweet, cakey, moist, and I felt enormous relief. I raised it to my mouth for a second bite, but in the maneuver it somehow leapt from my hand and danced away from me, a sprightly polka, dum de dum de dum, bouncing down my navy-blue A-line, one bright pink spot of icing, then a second, then a third, then a fourth, evenly spaced down my front.

I would like to say that I died, or fainted, or even better, that my derring-do, ending so ignominiously in disaster, brought smiles to all of our lips, so that words flowed and fast friendships were begun there in the headmaster's sun room, but none of those things happened. The others said nothing, pretended not to notice, while I stayed rooted to my spot by the table. Eventually the headmaster's wife came in. She made her way around the room discreetly, perhaps leaving us hapless ones for the end; her eyes seemed even more tired than they had at the front door. "Where are you from?" "Are you unpacked?" "Did your parents drive up last night or this morning?" She made bright small talk and we each replied — we were, after all, capable of that — and then finally, mercifully, we were set free.

Outside, the sun had gone down, but inside that bright room filled with plants, I hadn't noticed. On subsequent days, the sun's descent behind the mountains was always one of my favorite sights. That night, however, it was merely suddenly dark, and the walk from the headmaster's house back to my dorm seemed unbearably long.

The next morning I arose to a bell and to more darkness. Eventually I would awaken each morning a few moments before the bell, but the darkness was a constant. We would rise to it most mornings, and the evening would come early, the sun in the winter disappearing shortly after four. In the pale light of our rooms, shrouded by the deep dark from outside that still felt like night, we all shivered out of bed, showered, washed our faces, and brushed our teeth. We put on the blouses with the Peter Pan collars and the sweater that came in several colors and one of the two lightweight skirts that comprised our school uniform in the fall — a selection of matching clothes in a choice of shades and two or three styles. On our feet we wore lace-up brogues from Abercrombie & Fitch that we called our "sturds," short for sturdy shoes.

I trudged with all of the other girls to the dining hall for breakfast where, after grace was said, one of us from each table lined up to procure our food. I trudged with all of them back to the dorm again, to clean my room for inspection, to do daily chores, to sweep the hallway or clean the bathroom, or to help tidy up one of the classrooms or the library. I made my way to the gym for job assembly, where the entire school sat up on bleachers, and were addressed by the senior girls known as prefects, who had been chosen to be our leaders at the end of the preceding year. Announcements were made, rules were explained, and punishments, known as hours — an hour of work such as raking leaves or scrubbing the kitchen floor for infractions of school rules — were meted out. Occasionally short skits were performed. From the gym I made my way to the schoolhouse, our classes' beginning and end, like everything else, signaled by the ringing of bells. The classes were small, usually no more than eight or nine students. We were to stand up when any adult entered the room.

My first few weeks went by in a daze of newness, seasoned by the homesickness that attacked me in waves. I stumbled from place to place, from the dorm to the schoolhouse to the gym to the dining room and back to the dorm again. People spoke, I spoke in return, but I have no recollection of anything that was said.

I felt both strangely visible and invisible. Except for a cook in the kitchen, who would smile at me when it was my turn to go and obtain our food, mine was the only brown face at the school. My color made me stand out and at the same time recede. I jumped back and forth in my consciousness: one moment aware of nothing but how I must look to the others, my singularity, and in the next moment tucked deep within myself, wholly unmindful of how I might look, a silent eye peering about. I wrote my parents nearly daily, circling and labeling the tear stains that collected on the pages. I phoned them and begged that they relent and let me come home, but they were adamant — I had made this decision myself, and now I would see it to its end.

My only other conscious task those first few weeks, besides this assault on my parents, was to search for the other Negro girl who was supposed to be here. When I had been told there would be two of us, I hadn't thought to ask her name. Apparently, whereas I was obviously a Negro, with my brown skin and chemically straightened hair, she was not so easy to spot. She must have light skin and naturally wavy or curly or straight hair, I thought, and each time the whole school was assembled, I scanned faces looking for her.

I was not sure what I would do with her when I found her, but it felt crucial to me that I unearth her. I wanted first just to stand beside her so that my singularity would end. I wanted the illusion of family. I wanted to look in her eyes and exchange a look — a look that acknowledged our sameness, our camaraderie, our jointly held position as one among two. It also seemed vaguely unfair that she should know right away who I was while I spent these first weeks so desperately searching. More than anything else, I wanted to feel part of a group, to be a member of something composed of more than just me.

I narrowed my search to three or four girls, each of them with thick, black, wavy hair, each of them ivory-skinned with a tinge of pale brown, each of them with features that I thought could go either way. By the end of two weeks I had further narrowed my search to two girls, the real Negro and another girl who I would later learn was Jewish. I had almost decided that the Jewish girl was the one, when my real racial comrade was finally revealed in a dorm room one night.

There were several girls gathered in the room talking: Charlene, one of the two "suspects" I had identified; Pam, who was from New York City; and two other girls who roomed in that dorm. I was walking back to my room from the soda machine when Pam called to me to come in. She'd gotten a care package from home and invited me to stay and have some crackers and cheese. Everyone was sprawled on the two beds, and I opted for the chair at a desk by the door.

"How did it feel, deciding to come to a school where there was only one other Negro girl?" Pam asked after I had been in the room for a short while, apropos of nothing that I could tell. She addressed this question to Charlene. Pam was nearly as tall as I was, with very long, thick, straight blond hair. She was an old girl and already well known throughout the school for her blunt and wisecracking ways.

Charlene laughed and leaned her head against the wall beside the bed.

"Nobody *told* me there'd be only us two," she said, acknowledging me just for a second as she spoke. Everyone laughed at her answer. No one turned to ask me how I might have felt, but it suddenly occurred to me that Charlene's answer was the right one. It implied trickery, chicanery, on the part of the school. It indicated that no one in her right mind would have gone to Kent had she known the truth of the situation. I realized, of course, that since I knew and chose Kent anyway, I must be lacking in some discernment that came naturally to Charlene. I told myself, Well, at least there will be two of us, and I was embarrassed at my naiveté. I wondered again how it was that I had managed to miss something so clear to everyone else.

It was merely a brief exchange, but from that moment on, a pattern was set in motion. Charlene, aided and bolstered by her friendship with Pam — who was cool and sarcastic and tough and, after all, from New York City, even though she was not a Negro — was the one people went to with questions about what it was like to be a Negro, what she thought about Negro issues, and Charlene always had a breezy or laconic or slightly bitter answer. She took no one seriously, including herself. She was easygoing, just a trifle caustic and ironic, and it was as if everyone knew right away that she was the real, official Negro, not me. When other girls wanted the definitive Negro opinion, it was Charlene whom they quoted. When they wanted to show they were cool, broad-minded, risqué, it was Charlene whom they wished to include. It was not clear what I was, but I was not an official anything.

For the second time in my life I realized that I was standing on a platform that was shaky at best. I had never had occasion to think about what being a Negro meant when colored people were my entire world, and now, upon leaving that world, I was told that as a Negro I did not, in some critical way, measure up. I was as wholly myself as any other somewhat shy and self-conscious fifteen-year-old, and yet in the space of a few moments it felt as if my one chance at distinction had been taken away. I was envious of Charlene, envious of her cool and breezy manner, envious of her seeming ability to both embody and be aloof from whatever it was other people expected.

If I was not to be Gwen the Negro, then I began to wonder who it was I would be.

All around me, everyone seemed to be sorting into groups at an alarming rate. I quickly discovered that there was a top at Kent, as there was at most schools, and that here, as among most teenagers, this top was composed of those who were "in." These were the most traditionally pretty girls, the tallest and most athletic boys, but it also included those who had money. What nature had not given, money often could buy. For the first time in my life I was among not just the comfortably prosperous, but people whose concept of money went well beyond my imagining. The preppies, the rest of us called them — the Muffys and Buffys and Biffs. The ones named Taylor and Bob and Morgan and Dick, with II's and III's and IV's, after their last names. Their parents made million-dollar donations to the school, they spent winter vacations in Switzerland or on some French Caribbean isle, they had been in boarding schools or private schools since they were five. Theirs was a position garnered by looks and money and ancestry, but it was secured with an attitude as well: for them, any other position was unthinkable, and they would and could take their place as easily as they slipped into their Saturday night shoes. Pappagallos, by the way, were the shoes of choice: slim, multicolored pumps in butter-soft leather, in impossible shades of pink married to lime green, and yellow matched with burgundy or cream. Little sisters joined the preppies' ranks in the next tier, cousins were ringed round the side. Those of us from mere families without a lineage found that there was no way we could compete. We did not say "Daddy" and "Mummy." We did not speak of houses, as in the country house, the house in the south of France. We said "Dad" and "my mother," and what we summered in was our one and only home. We betrayed ourselves each time we spoke, but oddly enough, I found the hierarchy built on this class distinction freeing.

In Mount Vernon, I had been made to feel that being Negro was a problem and that the rest of the world was a cozy whole from which only people like me were excluded. But now I was learning that there was no such clear dividing line. In fact, there were no simple notions of haves and have nots, of black versus white. Instead, I saw that the world was splintered into innumerable factions and cliques and castes, that there were endless distinctions that people, if given the chance, drew among themselves. It also made me see that positions in life were not fixed, but rather were a matter of context. Being richer or poorer or higher in status was always a matter of being richer or more privileged than *whom?*

Even better, by taking up the top slot so completely, so utterly, the preppies made a lot of breathing room for the rest of us. They were the ones whose fortunes could rise and fall, who could lose their standing in a subtle way and feel they had fallen from grace. Below them came the mere jocks and the hearty. Well fed, healthy, and outgoing, they laughed all the time, were always breathless as they ran in from a great game in the field. They seemed unaffected by life, as if nothing could ever disturb them. They were named good solid things like Debbie and Susie and Kate. They did not brood or become introspective. If not the best looking, they were sturdily attractive.

Below the jocks were the determinedly cool. Attractive and wealthy enough to be in the upper tiers, they willingly chose exile, as if they couldn't be bothered. They were angry and sarcastic and flippant. When they wanted to, they could move up a notch. And below them were all the others: the unrich, the unjock, the uncool. I was not the official Negro, just the brown one. I was not popular or cool. I was unidentified, unaffiliated, but there were enough of us at the bottom that I soon relished being just one among a faceless crowd of nobodies, somebody who was not popular enough for anyone else to notice or make a fuss about.

I enjoyed my anonymity, the space that it returned to me. Days would go by and I did my homework and ate my meals and sat at assembly, and I realized that no one's eyes were on me. Whatever curiosity value I had initially possessed ended quickly when people learned I had no exciting Negro stories to tell. I had nothing to add by virtue of this status, and beyond that, there was nothing particular to make me stand out. Instead, I was mainly left alone. I could think my own thoughts, wander about with some poem or story alive in my head, and no one was there to push or jostle me, no one to be mad about what grade I got on a test. And the teachers, an eclectic lot, were for the most part the kind of people who would also have been in the lowly group had they gone to the school. They were misfits by teenagers' standards, as well as by the pecking order of the world outside, earning neither much money nor much status for the jobs they did. Still, most of the teachers tackled their jobs with love and with pride. They had their own reasons for being here, and they showed only an absent-minded interest in who our parents were, or who it was that the world said we should be.

After the early months of homesickness and trepidation over my position as "one among two" at Kent, I felt myself begin to relax as I had not relaxed since we left Durham. Though my station was lowly, I liked being among a small group of people again, of having my boundaries fixed and known, and living within a community that was intimately tied together, no matter how disparate its elements. I liked the noise and the rhythm of living with others, the knowledge that accrued silently, as habits were observed and accommodated. I eventually stopped writing the tear-stained letters to my parents. The days did not seem interminable any longer.

*　　　*　　　*

More than anything, what Kent returned to me was the reliving of my first love affair — namely, my love for the physical world. Kent was, if nothing else in those first few months, a place of breathtaking beauty. Although the South had held me in its arms like a sweaty lover, the top of Skiff Mountain overwhelmed me with its drama and changing face and slapped me awake. The trees were so bright in the fall that they screamed, everywhere a blaring of color. Winter's coming was stark, ominous, sculptural, the trees stripped to their essence, the light a pearly blue at dawn. While the boys' school had the river and the hills surrounding it, and the graceful splendor of its old Georgian buildings, the girls' school was merely functional and new. But oh, the view! The ride to the top of the mountain where the girls' campus perched was harrowing, along a narrow winding road that threatened all traffic in the icy winter. But when you emerged, it was as if the air itself had fallen in love with the place. The valley revealed itself only surreptitiously, here and there through a break in the trees or the plateau, so that it suddenly opened below in a great vertiginous rush. At night the pitch-black sky, lanced with stars, appeared so close we believed we might touch it with our tongues. The mist that shrouded the whole mountaintop in the morning was thick enough to drink. Each sunset and sunrise was a brazen display.

All of us, I think, were touched by this beauty that so casually became a part of our day: the sunlight that blanketed us in a sea of gold in the middle of a clear day, the icy cold, the profligate coming of spring. Though the official policy was that work and rules and shared rituals would bind us into one, the sense of community it endeavored to foster was first really knitted together by the seduction of the landscape.

As it had been in Durham, the physical world again became a companion and friend whose passion could always be counted on to match my own. I loved the wide-open feeling of the mountain, the sheer dizzying view from the library where you truly had a sense of the awesome height, and the moonlight as it glanced off the skating pond out in a field beyond the dorms at night. I was no good at any sport except basketball, and then only by virtue of the advantage my height gave me, but just running the length of a sparkling green field was delight enough for me.

By the second term, I even began to make a few friends. None were particularly popular, none made me the center of their world, but I was accepted and liked, and I enjoyed the company of a few, including a quiet girl with long brown hair who had shared the room of misery with me that first day at the headmaster's. By now, for most of the time, my race seemed of little consequence to the girls who were interested in a friendship with me, and those to whom it did matter now had a dozen other reasons for rejecting me. Some of the indifference to race was simply a function of class: there was just not that much dissimilarity among those of us who were "the middle-class girls" — our parents had the same kinds of jobs, our homes had the same types of comforts. We sorted ourselves much more along the lines of temperament and interests. As the weeks flowed into months, our studies and sports and chores and chapel kept us busy. For spare time, I had my books, my thoughts, my few friends, and the mountaintop itself to enjoy.

During the spring of my first year, I was approached by one of the English teachers at the boys' school, who was also the head of the drama department, to audition for a part in a play. As shy as I was, I don't think it would have occurred to me to try out if I hadn't been asked. However, his reason for asking me became readily apparent when I found out what play had been chosen — *In White America,* by Martin Duberman, a series of vignettes depicting the history of the Negro in the United States. I was cast to play all of the Negro women and girl parts. Two white boys would play all of the white male roles. One of the boys was a senior named Ted Danson, who would become well known one day for his part as the TV bartender in *Cheers.* Charlene's friend Pam, the tough-talking New Yorker, was cast as the female white lead. A Negro boy completed the cast.

The play opened with the beginning of the slave trade and used historical documents to re-create various scenes and dialogue concerning the Negro's fraught journey in white America. I played slaves, the abolitionist Sojourner Truth, and anonymous voices of black women. In a climactic scene, I was the fifteen-year-old girl who integrated the first school in the South, in Little Rock, Arkansas. It was the longest speech in the play, and for much of it I was on the stage alone, walking slowly across it in a pool of light. Invisible in the shadows was the specter of jeering, taunting crowds that actually had met that young girl as she walked toward the door of the school.

I had no technique as an actor except to pretend it was real, and so, for the few performances we gave, I became that young girl, in the freshly ironed new dress that she had made to wear on the first day of school, facing the fears that were, in reality, a starker and graver version of my own. Looking back on it, I realize that the irony of the situation was totally lost on me: I did not once think of this experience as in any way paralleling my own. I simply was that girl, walking so carefully, her desire for acceptance suffusing her every move, her hopefulness expressed in her excitement as she awoke in the morning, and in her naive belief that the National Guard troops would protect her. Nightly, I felt the surprise and sharp sting of rejection that I imagined she had felt when those same troopers closed ranks with their bayonets, protecting not her but the school, and the same growing fear, still mixed with disbelief, as the crowd moved menacingly toward her. A face she imagines to be friendly suddenly screams at her and spits, and now, almost as if her feet were moving on their own, the young girl makes her way to a bench, which she imagines will hold some measure of safety. When she gets there, as the crowd shouts to lynch her, a white man appears and sits down next to her and puts his arm around her as she cries.

I can still recall the feelings the play evoked in me, the tears that I cried every night when we rehearsed and then performed the play, and the rush of sweet and urgent release that swept over me when Ted Danson, as the white man, sat down next to me and put his arm around my shoulder. I would learn later that on opening night the audience was in tears as well — students, parents, teachers, even the director of the play, who ran backstage after it was over and hugged me. But when I sat on that bench I was lost in a dream, my own anguished hope that indeed there might be kindness in the world after all. My teenage accommodation to casual cruelty was to pretend not to notice, not to care. I willed myself to forget how much I yearned for the reverse to be true. The play took me back, nightly, not to the stones and jeers that that young girl had faced, but to distant eyes and people turning their backs on me and voices that didn't want to include me in their circle of humanity. It also took me back to the time when that had not been so, and then forward to a mythical and dreamed-for future when it would be that way again. Mixing my feelings all around in my mind, I developed a brief and intense crush on Ted, as if he were the deliverer of this world. I watched him from the wings as he said his other lines, and I built up, each time we rehearsed it, the moment that was about to come, when he would sit down next to me and put his arm around me. It was the moment for which, without even knowing it, I'd been waiting so long — that perfect moment when distance and hatred would disappear, when all the categories that locked us away from each other would melt away, and we would no longer be a white boy and black girl, but just two people giving and receiving kindness in the gravest and most perfect communion.

It would have been the most natural thing in the world if the play had engendered more conversations about race at the school — an effect, that, I can see now, the teacher was valiantly seeking. But we were teenagers, and this was a play, so whatever anxieties were raised about the large role that race would in fact play in all of our lives went underground. My own hopes went underground, as did my dreams of release. Whatever tears were shed, and hugs were shared, their effects were only privately known.

After my first year at Kent, my life settled into a routine. I continued playing basketball, and after my initial foray with drama, was involved in it for the rest of my time at the school. I had my few friends — Libby, who kept voluminously detailed journals; K.C., the artistic one with a rib-shattering wit; another Pam, not the New Yorker, this one a math and science whiz with the look of disgust that could wither. The only enemy I could say that I had was Mrs. Owens, the dean of girls.

I never really understood her antipathy toward me. In her view, it appeared the world was a combative and treacherous place. She seemed happiest when she was delivering a lecture to us on such things as the ways of men, of whom she did not have a high opinion. During these lectures we girls all giggled and whispered. "You may think you look good with your skirt rolled up to here, but you do not see yourself retreating," Mrs. Owens would warn.

"But Mrs. Owens," I asked her one day, "what if you look good retreating?"

Everyone laughed, and I think it was then that she began to dislike me. Others she did not like gave her more rope with which to hang them, but I never crossed over that line. She always accused me of lying to her, when the truth was that I almost never did. I liked the clarity of "hours." Do a deed, get caught, take your hours in punishment. It seemed cleaner and more honest that way. But if anything, my refusal to lie seemed to bother Mrs. Owens even more than the fact that I had broken a rule. If I was caught up after lights out, I would simply admit I'd wanted some hot chocolate, or that I hadn't been sleepy and had gone to chat with some friends. This always incensed Mrs. Owens. "You are not even sorry," she would snarl.

One day during my fifth-form (junior) year, there was a dinner dance at Kent with another boys' school. I hadn't signed up for the dance, but so few girls had that Mrs. Owens ordered the whole fifth form to go. Some of us talked about wearing the most repulsive clothes we could find, but when the Saturday night came, we all dressed as we normally did.

My date was a Negro boy, slim with pinched features. It was what I had grown to expect, since if there was ever a Negro boy at any of these dances, Charlene or I were always assigned as his date. This particular boy was quiet, but not in a shy way, just aloof and somewhat haughty. When he finally deigned to talk to me, he displayed a disdainful opinion of girls. "That's just like a girl," he sniffed several times. When I asked him about some of his classes, he laughed at my questions as if I were stupid. By the end of dinner I actively disliked him. I was also dreading having to dance with him. I was a tolerable dancer when I danced on my own, but when a partner tried to lead me, I grew clumsy and unable to follow. I hoped that he wouldn't like to dance, that instead we could sit on the side and watch, the loud music relieving us of any necessity to talk.

But as it turned out, he liked to dance, and he dragged me out onto the floor as soon as the music started. It was not a slow song, but he took me in his arms as if it were slow. He pressed his face against mine, his skin hot and sweaty, his breath so close that I could feel it like a hair dryer, blowing on my cheek and neck. I tried to stand a little way apart, to put some distance between us, but he was not aloof now. I was too embarrassed to push him away, so I just stood there as he held me tightly. The first dance ended and another one began.

"Excuse me," I said, "I have to go to the bathroom."

I made my way to the back of the gym, where the bathrooms were, and looked out to the dance floor when I came out. The dancing area was created by a tent put up in the gym, setting off the rafters and the bleachers and the hardwood floor with red and blue lines, making it look like a place that it wasn't. Inside the tent there was music and soft lights and tables and all of the other boys and girls dancing. Outside was just the gym, and beyond that the dorms. I had heard about girls leaving a dance before — you didn't like your date, or he didn't like you. It was done all the time. So I fled for the night air, away from that stranger who was intent on pressing against me, back to my dorm and my friends.

Nearly two hours passed. The dance was about at its end. I had changed my clothes and was in a friend's room, lounging on a dorm bed, eating crackers and smoked oysters she'd gotten in a package from home. Then I heard footsteps, running fast, too fast, down the hall. Another friend of mine burst in, one from my own dorm.

"Gwen," she said breathlessly, "Mrs. Owens is looking for you."

For a moment I was confused. Mrs. Owens was one of the chaperones. She was at the gym, seated at the head table or else prowling the sides of the dance floor, searching out couples who might have retreated to a dark corner in which to kiss or touch. How could she be looking for me?

"Back at the gym?" I asked.

"No," my friend said wildly. "At the dorm, she's in the dorm. She's going through all of them, calling your name, asking everyone have they seen you."

If the showers had had more than short curtains, if the beds had been higher, with longer spreads that swept to the floor, if there had been anyplace reliable that I could have gone to hide, I would have run there, but there was no use in running. Everything was designed so that none of us would be lost or misplaced, so that our chastity could be reliably maintained, and that meant no place to run or hide. It would have been useless anyway. I heard the dorm doors open at the end of the hall, the *click click click* of high heels that could only be a teacher's.

She was in the room before anyone had a chance to move, to try and hide the food we were not supposed to keep in our rooms, to get to our feet the way we were supposed to do when an adult came into the room.

"Gwen Parker," she said, flinging my name like a curse. "Get up from there."

If it had been allowed by the school, I think she would have slapped me. Her face was strangled and purple with rage.

"Get up right this instant!"

I stood up, and she moved toward me as if she might yank my arm, but she didn't touch me.

"Go to your room. Change back into your Saturday night," she yelled. "Right away." I started walking and she kept pace behind me, still yelling. "Hurry up! You have disgraced this school and yourself. When you are dressed, you will come straight to the head table at the gym to apologize."

I arrived at my room and Mrs. Owens left. My friends trailed in after me. They didn't speak. They all filed into my room and watched me quickly change back into my Saturday night. "Boy, she was mad," one of my friends eventually said.

"Jesus, Parker," someone else said, "what did you do?"

I really didn't know. I walked back across the campus, the stars, as always, a brazen display. It was like velvet outside, and almost despite myself, I felt the night trying to take me away.

I made my way to the head table. Mrs. Owens was there,

Mr. Towle and his wife were there, the math teacher, the Greek teacher, the history teacher, the English teacher — a small sea of round white faces.

"You will apologize to all of us," Mrs. Owens hissed. "You will say you are sorry for disgracing Kent School. And then you will apologize to your date for being so phenomenally rude."

I hadn't seen him at first, but I saw him now. He was standing by the head table, almost in shadow. I wondered what he had done. Had he asked another girl to dance, and pressed against her that way, had that been what had caught their attention? Or had he merely stood on the side, slim and hot and brown, like a flashing light? Dozens of girls had left dances before, dozens at a time, hundreds over the course of a year. No one else had ever been captured and brought back. No one else had ever been made to return and say she was sorry.

I looked at all of them waiting. Mrs. Owens's face was nearly triumphant with glee. I realized then that she may have disliked me for several reasons, but chief among them was my audacity in believing I was entitled to do what I wanted. There was, in her mind, a great pecking order, and only those at the very top were deeded the privilege of inhabiting their desires and feeling at ease to express themselves in the world. And this very top was composed of people who possessed very specific characteristics, none of which I possessed. Yet in her view I clung stubbornly to an irrepressible image of myself. And it was this about me — so irritatingly packaged in my lowly female brown skin — that Mrs. Owens so despised.

She had got me, her eyes told me. I would say what she wanted. I would finally be bent to her will.

I looked at Mrs. Owens again, and at the rest of the people

at the table, who were also eating, and waiting. And even though I could feel my palms sweaty at my side, I still didn't speak right away. I chose my words carefully.

"I'm sorry you feel my leaving disgraced the school," I said to Mrs. Owens slowly. I then looked at my date. "I'm sorry you were upset that I left," I told him.

I could see Mrs. Owens catching the words like a bouquet at a wedding, only to discover that she had caught nothing but a bundle of weeds. She looked angrily at the others, who were now paying scant attention to me. Besides, it was late, whatever the row was about. Mrs. Owens looked one last time at Mr. Towle to see if she could find at least one ally, but he was also through with the subject.

I could see her starting to fume. I hadn't really apologized, but no one else seemed to care. Besides, the lights were starting to flash, signaling that the dance was over. The teachers hurriedly finished their coffee. Mrs. Owens reluctantly released me, and I went slowly with my date out to the bus.

As I walked through the night, I thought of the moment when I'd heard Mrs. Owens's high heels, and the look of fury on her face when she'd found me. And then I thought of the table filled with teachers and her dragging me to it. I understood that though her rage and disapproval had made me uncomfortable, I hadn't been afraid. Moreover, I saw that while she could feel one way, I had feelings of my own I could possess. I hadn't said what she wanted, and I exulted in that. As nervous as I'd been, still it wasn't I who'd been wrong. After that night, Mrs. Owens was never able to upset me in the same way again.

*   *   *

As the last spring before graduation arrived, I could feel everything drawing to a close. My seclusion from the rest of the world, the friendships that were now as close as family, those nights up after hours, talking and laughing, all of those mornings studying at the schoolhouse — who, after all, would be up at four-thirty to see the dozen or so of us who made our way over there, the Breakfast Club we called ourselves, those of us who found dawn an easier time to study than night — they were all coming to an end.

Besides, by now we were all chafing to leave. Everything had been done too many times before. How many times could we eat crackers and smoked oysters and giggle? How many times could I dance with friends? People were applying and hearing from colleges, and the great sorting out was beginning again. Where are you going? Where have you been admitted? What is your safety school?

Up until then, I had been a good student in all of my classes, but not the best in anything. I was not a math whiz like Pam, not the artist like K.C., not the literary genius like David, who set T. S. Eliot and Ezra Pound poems to music. Even my one abiding passion, writing, was still my private joy. All that had cohered was that I still submerged myself in the natural and sensory world every chance I got, still was too curious about everything and everybody, and community, even one as flawed as this one, still moved me.

We approached the end of the year, and just as it had on the day I arrived, everything began to acquire a patina — the last time, the last time.

The senior dance was the final time the dining hall and the gym would be transformed. The loudspeakers blared the Animals' "We Gotta Get Out of This Place," and we all screamed as if it were an anthem. I sat with all of my friends: Eric Jensen, nicknamed Rock Luster, who would grow up to be a music professor; David, who would become an English professor at Brown; "Disco" Dan, who only at the age of thirty would allow himself to wear nice clothes; K.C., who would become a graphic designer; Libby, who would work on computer manuals by day and on her own books at night. From a bunch of strangers, we had been ground down to people who didn't always like one another, but knew each other well. My father had wanted me to have lobster and shrimp, and know who Matisse was and Frank Lloyd Wright, and not ever to be intimidated by anything foreign or new. He got that wish and more — among many things, I understood that whatever white people might think of themselves, and whatever they might think of me, I knew them as well as they knew themselves. I would always be able to turn my head to the left or right and see the confident boss who thought he owned the world. I'd know who he was, where he'd come from, what kind of training he'd had. It gave me a freedom and a burden: the freedom of knowing I was everyone's equal, and the burden of knowing that as well.

When the final sorting out was over, one thing hadn't changed, however, and that was my facility for taking tests. I took the SAT and surprised all of my teachers with my good scores on both the math and the verbal. I had even done better than a lot of the students everyone thought were the best.

With my scores, my grades, and my prep school education, every college was open to me, just as my father had always hoped. He had urged me to aim for the top, and I had. I was accepted at Radcliffe College — the sister school to Harvard University — Stanford, the University of Pennsylvania, and my safety school. One teacher reacted with open-faced surprise at my acceptance at Radcliffe, and then I told him my SAT scores. There they were in black and white and supposedly neutral. The teacher was forced to admit that I had won my place fair and square. It was my very last lesson from Kent: when it came to prejudice, hard numbers could not be reckoned away.

I had applied to Radcliffe only because it was considered the best school in the country for women, and now that I had gotten in, it seemed as if I had no choice but to go. A place like Harvard, like Radcliffe, my father argued, will open doors for you for the rest of your life. More importantly for me, it removed one more barrier that I might encounter in life. Some people might not want me to be bright, they might want anything else to be true, but I had this additional chip in my pocket, and it was not something they could ever take away.

FOUR

Climbing the Ivy

My GRANDMOTHER PARKER came along when my parents delivered me to Radcliffe College in the fall of 1968. She was wearing one of her best dresses, her hair freshly done, her jewelry in place. We drove slowly along the tree-lined streets of Cambridge that led to Radcliffe's buildings and dorms so that she could see the Harvard campus with its Yard and its many quadrangles. We drove through Harvard Square, crammed full of students with green book bags slung over their shoulders and stores and restaurants sporting Harvard memorabilia. Once at Radcliffe and out of our car, my grandmother stayed close to me. Occasionally she took hold of my arm, as if she were frail and in need of assistance. But her grip belied that. It was firm and steely, and her legs, even on the uneven sidewalks, never wavered a bit.

We did not speak of her father, but he was like a ghost at her side. I knew she was conjuring him up, showing him the sights that we saw. Born a slave, freed by the Emancipation when he was six, he'd worked hard and long his whole life so that his people would have as much as the world could offer. Grandmother Parker didn't need to tell me how fiercely proud he would be now that his great-granddaughter was attending one of the best universities in the country. It was the ful-fillment of everything he, and she as the carrier of his legacy, had ever talked about: the need for the colored, as she still sometimes called our people, to be able to go anywhere that white people went, to prove to them what we were capable of; the absolute crucialness of education and the importance of amassing as much of it as possible, and from the finest institu-tions one was able to attend; and the determination to follow, without pause, the trajectory that led only one way, upward, forward, toward success. He started out with nothing, she must have told me dozens, hundreds of times. By the time he died, he had built four houses, one for each of his children; he owned a string of grocery stores; he was at the center of local politics and looked everyone in the eye, as an equal.

"This doesn't surprise me," my grandmother said to me as we made our way toward my dorm, pulling me even closer to her with her fierce grip, and with her free arm waving about her, indicating the school. "Not one bit." And then she pulled me closer still. "I always knew you were smart," she said tersely. "Always."

My father and I carried my things upstairs while my mother began hanging clothes in the closet. My grandmother stood in my room, peering out into the hall. My dorm room was only about half the size of my room at Kent, with an iron double bed in one corner and two small old desks at the end of the room. The closet my roommate and I would share was narrow though deep. She arrived as we were just about finished unpacking and introduced herself. Her name was Nancy and she seemed pleasant, a white girl with medium-length brownish hair and a long oval face whose last name I can no longer recall. My father approached her eagerly, peppering her with questions. He was clearly excited, in a way more excited than I was. Ever since my older brother and I had started looking at colleges, I knew that this was a dream of his — that his children, any or all three of us, should attend an Ivy League school. And now my older brother was a junior at the University of Pennsylvania, and I was starting at Harvard. To him, these small bare walls supported a tradition and a lineage of which I would be a part.

My mother, by contrast, was quiet and seemed uncomfortable, as if this taking leave of her children never got any easier. She had earned her master's degree from Columbia decades ago, and I wondered if she was remembering her own transitions away at school, particularly the phone call that had come when she was nineteen, telling her that her father had suddenly and unexpectedly died.

When it was time to go, my grandmother squeezed my hand as I walked them all to the car. She said she didn't need to tell me to study hard, because she knew that was what I would do. My mother cried and hugged me tightly, and even my father, as he gave me a fast hug goodbye, had tears in his eyes. After they were gone, I stood at one corner of Radcliffe Yard, just beyond the shadow of my dorm.

From the little cloistered campus of some two hundred girls at Kent, chaperoned and supervised in every area of life, I was being set down in an incomprehensibly large, unruly, and sprawling campus that was like a small city, with not a single adult charged with monitoring my comings and goings.

I had left Kent feeling secure, cocky even, as if life from

here on out would be as simple and unruffled as it had been for those three years. I had felt, by the time I left there, sure of my place within its close boundaries. And now I had to admit that the world was not nearly so manageable as I had thought. In fact, I sensed that what I knew of it was not nearly enough, and that my place within it was impossibly small. Most acutely I felt that I had been charged with a task: to conquer this world, to reemerge from my cocoon and live up to all of the dreams that had brought me to this place. At my core, I felt wholly inadequate to the task. I feared I did not have the steely determination of my grandmother Parker. After all, I had not seen or known firsthand the things that she and her father had seen. Unlike their sure legs, mine would surely falter. Whatever skills this place was going to require, these were precisely the ones I feared I lacked.

There were 316 girls in my class at Radcliffe, 1,210 in the freshman class at Harvard. Among the incoming class were approximately eight black girls, proportionally not even as many as at Kent, but enough of us to form at least the semblance of a group. In the class before mine, there had been about the same number.

I met most of them at a social that was organized by the returning students to welcome their younger black sisters. It was held in the lounge of my dorm, and the group was small enough that the gathering felt like an intimate party at somebody's home. It was the first time I remember being addressed as "sister," and I liked the resonance of it, ushering me as it did into a familial space with these strangers. Three of the returning students in particular would befriend me: Suzanne Lynn, Octavia Hudson, and Lani Guinier.

Suzanne was light-skinned and freckled, with a bright, coppery bush of hair. It seemed the perfect counterpoint to her personality, which was emotional, quick-tempered, hotheaded. She was bright, impulsive, and funny. Suzanne's father was Conrad Lynn, a civil rights attorney and activist who, along with William Kunstler, was known for his participation in the defense of the Harlem Six — young boys in a pigeon club who had been charged with a robbery and murder many believed they did not commit. Suzanne seemed to have arrived at college — at least now in her second year, when I met her — knowing exactly what she would do and who she would be. She wanted to be a civil rights lawyer like her father. She had read Frantz Fanon and Che Guevara, and though she had flirted with interracial politics for a while, having been a member of the largely white radical group Students for a Democratic Society, she was now totally committed to black people and their struggle.

Lani Guinier was similarly sure of herself, but without Suzanne's hot-headedness and biting tongue. She was a model of reason. Whenever tempers threatened to flare, Lani would use logic and analysis to persuade. She was not only self-assured, but sure of others: she accorded everyone the benefit of her respect. Even in the midst of arguments and debates, Lani's method was to assume your good intentions and your intelligence. If there were any errors in your thinking, her manner conveyed, you would come to realize them on your own once you had the requisite information. Like Suzanne, Lani came with impeccable credentials as a bona fide leader in the making. Her father was a history professor at Columbia and was later appointed the first chair of Afro-American Studies at Harvard, and she too seemed to have spent no time doubting who or what it was she would be.

Octavia was a natural-born leader as well. She had a regal, self-confident air about her. She was always stylishly dressed, and with her burnished dark skin and good sense of humor she reminded me a little of my cousin Louise. As I would learn later, she was one of the student leaders of Afro, the Association of African and Afro-American Students, and she was also the dorm mother. She was the perfect mother for us girls: solicitous but somewhat distant, she gave us the nudge that we needed when the time came to leave the nest.

There were others in the circle, who I would come to know cursorily, whose names I would see years later on the masthead of a magazine or in the pages of a newspaper announcing their appointment to some high post, others who would sit nightly with us at the round table in the same dining room, but Octavia and Suzanne and Lani were the ones I looked up to, the ones who did most of the talking, the ones everyone, including me, wanted to be like. Evenings, after studying was done, were spent in the basement of our dorm, playing cards until all hours of the night. But it was the talk and the conviviality that I most enjoyed.

I had never become part of a group so fast. I had made friends elsewhere, but they had been hard won, and here I was provided with instant credentials. I quickly assumed the stance of younger sister, not because I was that much younger, but because I felt young in terms of my exposure to life, and especially my awareness as a black sister — the phrase spoken with a slightly defiant ring.

Initially, at those basement and dinner discussions, I was

primarily a listener. I paid attention to what was said, and later looked for the books that I heard others mention. I had never been particularly interested in history or political theory, but I read those books now, the ones that were the currency of the day. *Soul on Ice* by Eldridge Cleaver, the plays of LeRoi Jones, who became Imamu Amiri Baraka, *The Autobiography of Malcolm X,* the works of Frantz Fanon. For me, the apogee of civil rights up until then had been the work and life of the Reverend Martin Luther King, Jr., and now, only a few short months after his assassination, I was meeting people who were critical of him and his methods. Integration as a goal was questioned. Appeals to principle and nonviolence as a tactic were critiqued. Even the merits of education were debated. Perhaps it was better, some argued, to make a revolution first.

A wave of militancy was also sweeping the campus, fueled by the turn away from the old civil rights vanguard as represented by Dr. King. A new spirit was ascending, that of the Black Power movement. The phrase was reportedly first used by Stokely Carmichael of the Student Nonviolent Coordinating Committee, and before long SNCC decided to oust the whites who for years had been active in the civil rights struggle. In time, the concept of Black Power was used as a tool of empowerment, giving to rural Southern blacks especially, who were the foot soldiers in the fight for black liberation, a means of taking control of their own lives, giving them the wherewithal to develop the leadership skills and self-confidence to lead their own struggle without being beholden to whites. The Black Power movement engendered many cultural shifts: using the word "black" rather than "Negro," and using it proudly, transforming what had been an epithet into a badge of pride;

eschewing the straightening comb and "process" chemicals, giving birth to the afro; and seeking not to assimilate into the white world but to embrace proudly the ways in which black people differed from whites.

It was a heady time, filled with heady notions. I remember being both exhilarated and taken aback by the idea that blackness itself should be exalted. On the one hand, being black was so much a part of who I was that it seemed a little like being proud of my ability to breathe. But it also provided a wedge, one that could be used to break up the logjammed notion so inherent in the dominant culture that only being white brought advantages and virtue. I was also caught up in the surface changes. I liked the word "black" — a color again, not the sterile, somewhat artificial-sounding word "Negro." I liked the freedom of my new afro hairstyle. I liked the feeling, too, that I was part of a movement, particularly one whose aim was to return to those who had lost it a sense of pride. I also liked the fact that this new solidarity meant that I instantly belonged, that without any real work I had a group — people to eat with, socialize with in the evening, hang out and talk with. I didn't have to hunt and peck to find the group; it was ready-made, and my membership had been guaranteed by the color of my skin. That I liked these girls, as I got to know them, just made it all the better. If all of these things were Black Power, then I liked it, too.

What was particularly satisfying was that I now had two groups: this new one and the old one of my friends from Kent. Three white friends from my Kent days went to Harvard, and several others were at Brown University in Providence. My friends at Harvard invited me down to their dorms when girls

were allowed, or we met for coffee or dinner in Harvard
Square, or they took me to Harvard house mixers and parties
that were always going on. Our friends at Brown, Brian and
Chuckie, had played in a band together at Kent, where, among
the strait-laced preppies, they were not wildly popular. But at
Brown they found their niche. Their dorm room was always
filled with people and music, with Brian seated like a Bedouin
Buddha in his tapestry-draped bed at the center. No longer
were we outcasts and weirdos — we were hippies, part of yet
another movement, based on freedom and music and love.

For my first semester at Radcliffe, I found a cozy comfort in
these two worlds. I was both a hippie and a participant in the
struggle for black liberation. Between discussions on how we
might best change the world, I took the usual freshman intro-
ductory classes, taught by famous professors who read from
their well-worn notes in an amusing and erudite fashion. I sat
at the back of the large lecture halls, intimidated by the sheer
number of students around me. When I studied quietly in my
room, the whole world was outside my window, beckoning
and threatening at the same time. I had my new Radcliffe
friends during the week and my Kent friends on the weekend,
and both worlds felt like family to me.

My two-footed straddle of those worlds did not last for long.
By the spring of 1969, the confrontational style of demonstrations that had swept other campuses came to Harvard. Our
conversations about justice, equality, and righteousness took
on more urgency. With everyone else from that time, I felt as if
I were not only at the edge of a new age, but that I would have
a part in shaping it. The image to me was clear: the new age we

would usher in would be free of hatred, free of cruelty, free of distinctions based on things as superficial as the color of one's skin or the region one was born in or the station in life one had been blessed with. It would contain, in a word, perfection. Every time I heard words like justice and peace and love and freedom and equality, I envisioned them true and in action, practiced and not just preached. If not today, then surely tomorrow, people would acknowledge their basic shared humanity, recognize how many more things they had in common than the things that kept them apart. It was what we all professed, but to me the ideals of the sixties were a tantalizing promise of a fruition that I believed I had once glimpsed and now wanted to see returned in a larger form. I had known community, flawed and isolated and imperfect, but it had been community, and in the deepest part of my heart I could not see why it would not be made whole and real for all of society, why people could not look into each other's souls and see the same desires that we all had and the same fears and the same hopes, and let that be the glue that would form community, not just shared oppression and skin tone and proximity.

It was perhaps naive to expect perfection from life, but my youth still betrayed me, and as I look back I realize that it is impossible to reenter that time without believing in the wish for true brotherhood and sisterhood, without digging back somewhere to find where we have buried that wish, and to unearth it, dust it off, and clasp it to ourselves once more, if only for a moment, allowing the sweet aroma of those hopes to drift into our nostrils and intoxicate us once again.

As group after group of students took action — taking over buildings, striking, and even, in the notorious photograph of students at Cornell, brandishing guns — what had once been mere words suddenly felt like palpable entities. We turned them over in our hands as if they were warm stones, and they lit up our eyes with their glow. In our youthful passion, we knew the course we set out on was the right one: we would run roughshod over the world that our parents had made and crumble it to dust underfoot. From the dirt we would gather up in our hands, we would make the world anew.

Harvard exploded with rallies, meetings, manifestoes. The culminating event was the takeover of University Hall by a group of mostly white students, who protested the war in Vietnam, Harvard's investment policies in South Africa, military recruitment on campus, and other issues. While the building was held, the rest of the students meandered in Harvard Yard, picking up leaflets, awaiting the news from inside. Early the next morning — it was April 9, 1969 — while most of us still slept, the police cleared University Hall. In the process, several students were injured, including a few blacks who had been mere onlookers. The leaders of Afro called an emergency meeting. It was during this heightened, overwrought event that I made the first move beyond my small circle of Radcliffe friends into the larger Harvard-Radcliffe black community.

The meeting was held in a basement lecture hall at Harvard. I was late in arriving, so the meeting was already well under way. As I squeezed in and found some standing room at the back of the hall, I was struck by the dizzying array of people and personalities in attendance. Here we were, a true cross-section of brown-skinned people, all united under this single new banner of Black Americans, and perhaps most strenuously united in our belief that we were, and our need to be, academically the best. The room was packed, the air was close and hot, and several people were talking at once. Several others stood at the front of the room trying to restore order and calm as an intense emotional fervor roiled from one end of the room to the other.

As I listened and looked around me, I found it hard to hold in mind that we were a singular anything. People began their sentences with "We this" and "We that," speaking of the need for unity, while the participants, it seemed to me, kept dissolving into their constituent parts. There were tweed jackets and flak jackets. Gold wire-rimmed glasses and dark shades. Jeans and tailored pants. Some people took the microphone and spoke as if they were only days away from becoming a professor. Others were already politicians, fiery and pithy, peppering their speech with phrases that sang. Some slouched against the wall as they spoke, keeping their dark glasses on, punching the air with their fists. Others accused and assailed. That we looked like a cornucopia of all the world's people, in a blizzard of shades and tones, didn't surprise me; I was accustomed to that. But the fact that there was almost no single experience that could be said to represent everyone's was surprising indeed.

I realized that I had no up-to-date picture of "blackness," not one that could stretch to take in this whole gathering. My experience with groups of black people had always been limited to a particular setting: Southern, familial, socially inbred. In Durham, not only the members but the hierarchy and pecking order were well known. Everyone knew everything about each other, even secrets they would have preferred to keep hidden. For the first time I was among a large group of blacks that felt as bewildering to me as any other large group. As with any group that was new to me, at first I couldn't easily fathom the rules and rituals. I didn't know what the norms and values were, who the leaders were and who was merely being tolerated, what the underlying consensus of the room might be.

My penchant for the personal also kept distracting my gaze. Just as a semblance of agreement on a theory or position was about to be reached, my attention would slide from the topic at hand to the hard ground of emotion and interpersonal dynamics underlying the speeches. When the discussion turned to the possible responses to the beating of the two students, for instance, on one side of the issue were arrayed the voices of protest. I likened them to the voices of old Southern black women, people like my grandmother and my great-aunts, who had seen more of human nature than they ever cared to know. It was protest tempered by an internal moral compass, an intimate knowledge of and grounding in right conduct that would always sustain them. In this meeting, such were the voices of people like Lani Guinier or Octavia Hudson, who inserted themselves when the pitch was rising too high.

These were familiar voices to me. They counseled moderation and reason, and aimed to reconcile both movement and preservation, not only of lives but of values. On the other side were voices that simply poured out grief and anger, the voices of people who were startled when confronted with what others were capable of doing, again and again. I recognized those voices as well, which were in many ways like my own. To these voices was added a new voice, which up until now I had heard only remotely, in books or on TV. It had no grounding in reality to me, as it had not originated in any experience with which I was familiar. In its original form, from those I would call the truly desperate, it was a voice ragged with pain and rage. It was a voice that knew no options, that was born in a cage and bred in a corner and lanced over by fear and callous violence.

As I heard it here, however, the voice struck me as filled with dissonance. When I'd heard it before — from Malcolm X, his father beaten by white men before his eyes; from young men living without hope or even the hope of hope, running down the streets of Detroit as flames licked at their feet — the voice made sense, and I believed it. But here, out of these well-fed, well-educated Harvard throats, I suddenly did not trust it.

"We ought to get some guns and show them how it feels!" one voice shouted.

"They need to know we're not going to take this shit lying down anymore," another said. "If they want to come at us with fists, then we'll meet them with fists. If they come at us with something more, then I'm with the brother too."

It was hyperbolic, swagger, righteous puffing up, like a snake getting ready to strike. And of course no one went out to buy guns. But the angry words spread from one mouth to another, and though the anger was undeniably real, there was something overblown about it. These boys are stealing rage, I told myself. They are appropriating a roar, claiming a history that was both theirs and not theirs.

And as I looked around the room, I saw other borrowings. Slouches on middle-class bodies that no doubt had been told to stand up straight from the time they were old enough to listen. Dark glasses veiling eyes that were pretending they had

•

something to hide. People speaking of a level of violence and oppression that merely their presence in this room had to belie.

I wondered why, why they would take on a mantle that was not their own. As I listened more, to the timbre that tried to echo the street, to the poses that were revealed as poses, to the deriding of the trappings of the educated, the scorning of the elite and the bourgeoisie, I saw that for some of these young brothers and sisters — the great majority of whom had come from homes as comfortable as my own — who they actually were did not feel authentic enough. They seemed to believe the popular notions about being black — that it encompassed precisely this experience and no more — and as a result, they could not sit easily enough within their own experience to claim it. This stealing of another's rage seemed ghoulish, as if these young men were anointing themselves for battle with other people's blood.

I tried to return my mind to the topic at hand — namely, what we as a group would do in response to the violence used by the police in removing the students from University Hall, and about the larger issues being pressed by SDS. Just as I began to listen intently again, a young man at the back of the room stood up. He had sandy, nearly blond hair, slightly wavy, and hazel eyes. He spoke rapidly and nervously.

"Take that microphone from him," someone from the side of the room shouted.

"Get that ofay out of here," another demanded.

A group of young men who were closer to him moved threateningly toward the light-skinned one who was speaking.

"This is a meeting for brothers and sisters only," one of the leaders announced. "I think you should leave."

As if to underscore the command, several men moved even closer, as if they were going to carry the offender out.

Just then a student standing near him came to the defense of the light-skinned young man: "He's a brother, he's a brother!"

Tempers cooled, but only slightly. The ones who had threatened to carry him out retreated, and there was a tepid exchange of handshakes. I watched the boy's face, now that he had been grudgingly accepted. He spoke, but there was a tenuousness in his voice, an almost imperceptible loosening of the ties that he had to the rest.

The meeting continued, and suggestions were turned over, debated, shouted down, but for me that young man's face loomed large. The sting of rejection in his eyes was like a merciless headlight that now shone on our appeals for unity and solidarity. The outlines of his face were the frame through which the notions of "black enough" were now viewed.

I realized that "blackness," to me, was many different things. It was a certain warmth in the voice when you welcomed someone to your house. It was wide-hipped and generous. It was always making sure someone had eaten. It was opening your home when needed. It was sitting on a stoop on a muggy hot day with a glass of iced tea dripping sweat on your hand. It was also a shared oppression, but the burdens of that had not been evenly distributed among all of our race, and among the black people I knew, that fact too had been recognized and acknowledged.

The blackness with which I was familiar was not the blackness that formed the substance of these new tests. This blackness had a hierarchy: some people had more of it than others, and those whose quota was found lacking could be challenged as to where their allegiances lay. This blackness would challenge or cast out those who did not fit a particular hue. And last, this blackness was not centered in its own experience, but seemed to require white people forever in the wings, poised as the listeners who had to be there to overhear what was said onstage.

As I left the meeting, I thought that much of my dislocation may have been the clash of North versus South, small town versus large city, or the difference between an identity formed in the absence of whites and that which had had to fight for every inch of its life. But I also felt an uneasiness that was hard to shake. What we college kids had to offer to a struggle would not, could not, be the same as that of our brothers and sisters whose lives were so vastly different from ours. We are lying to ourselves if we try to pretend to be something we are not, I kept thinking. And there was a corollary to that: it would only be from a place of truth, about who it was that we genuinely were, that we could ever hope to find something within ourselves that would be useful to this struggle we were taking on.

Several weeks after that meeting I had a different experience with some of my brothers from Afro. It was a distinctly personal experience, having nothing to do with the topics or goals of the group, but it was also indicative of the times. It would grow to be an unchallenged hegemony that part of the new Black Power ascendancy was a needed reassertion of "black manhood." The effect on black womanhood of such a rise, however, was nowhere discussed.

I was walking down the street with a new white friend of mine named Chester. Chester was a loopy boy who lived exclusively in a world composed of his own symbols and meanings. I met him through a Kent friend of mine who was his roommate. Chester was smart and eccentric and more than a little bit strange, but he was gentle and funny, and at the time we found a common conversational ground in our interests in Jungian psychology and mysticism and art. He was just a beginning friend, and we were threading our way from Harvard Square to Elsie's, a local sandwich shop. As we crossed a narrow street, a window above us opened and someone yelled out, "Hey, sister, sister."

I looked up, only half expecting it to be someone calling to me. I saw two black boys leaning out of the window. I couldn't recall their names, but I recognized them from an Afro meeting. I looked around the street, but there was no one else to whom they seemed to be calling. So I looked back up at them, smiled, and waved hello in return.

"What are you doing walking with that white devil?" one of the boys asked me in a jovial tone.

"Yeah, sister," the other boy added, shaking his head from side to side. "We're disappointed in you." They continued to shake their heads, slowly, as if I were a child they were gently scolding. Then one of them leaned farther out of the window, so that he could take in Chester as well.

"Are you sucking that white boy's dick?" he asked me, staring at Chester.

Chester made some sort of nonsensical response, ineffectual and meaningless. I didn't say anything at all. My feet started moving on their own, carrying me quickly away. I was wearing bell-bottoms that were too long, and a fringed poncho that restricted my arms. I felt as if I had no balance at all, but my feet wouldn't stop. I thought to myself that if I only moved fast enough, I would leave the moment behind. It would recede to a time that was further than past. My posture during the episode was humiliating: my face upturned, the two of them leaning down and out, as if flicking a piece of trash onto the street.

What I mostly reeled from was the color. These were brown faces — the tone, to me, of family, of trust. These boys were like my cousins, whose families were connected with mine. They would grow soon into the men I had known at our church. They would grow up to be my father's friends, live next door to me and grow tomatoes in the yard next to mine. They might tease me a little, say something goofy or silly, but they would never try to hurt me, never mean to hurt me in this way. For an instant I thought maybe I hadn't heard what I'd heard, but Chester repeated the words, abstractly to himself, turning them over as if they were something he would now examine.

Chester and I reached Elsie's, took a seat in a booth, and ordered mammoth roast beef sandwiches that I always had to take half the meat out of in order to eat. My stomach felt queasy. I didn't know how to protect myself from assaults like these. I had learned how to keep white people from hurting me, by being cautious and quiet and waiting to see who they were, but this kind of cruelty was new. It slashed me to the bone. I thought about going back and explaining that Chester and I were just friends, that he wasn't my boyfriend, but I knew that that wasn't the issue. In fact, when I replayed the moment, I saw that I was largely irrelevant. The current had run between Chester and them. If sparks singed me as they flung their challenge to him, I was just grass that was too dry at the side of the road.

This kind of verbal assault on me for the crime of walking down the street with a white happened countless times after that, though this first time stuck in my mind as the most graphic and crude. It was always a conversation among men. My walking with a white girl did not arouse the looks or the comments, and it was never girls who had something to say; it was a male-to-male contest, with me off to the side. Some boys just gave me a look, a little shake of the head that said, "Now, shouldn't you be ashamed." "Sister, sister," they sometimes would cluck, as if they could shame me back into the fold. Other times it was "Sister, you shouldn't be with that honky," this said nonchalantly, as if it were "Have a nice day." Sometimes I would try and anticipate the comments, steel myself for them, or through some silent pleading try to ward them off. When I saw a group of black boys approaching, I would make eye contact first, say hello, as if this would throw them, as if they wouldn't then notice who it was I was walking with. Sometimes I would keep my head down, pretend I didn't see them or hear them. Or I would combine the two, a look away and then a quick pleading look, as if I were saying, "See, really, I am nice, don't be mean to me, please, I'm asking nicely."

This cleaving of worlds was painful. I wanted all of my friends to like each other, I wanted my life to be all of a piece, and it was never that way at Harvard. One of the dining halls was the worst. It was not associated with any of the houses. It was near the classrooms and anyone could go there for lunch. It was a major gathering place, and anyone you knew might be there. Sometimes I went in and saw only one person I knew, so choosing a seat would be easy. Sometimes there was a group of black students and no white students I knew. More than once, however, I had to make choices, and I made them in an almost desperately random fashion — whoever it was I made eye contact with, whoever it was sitting closest to the front or the back, that's where I sat.

One crowded lunchtime, I joined several of my black friends at a long table. Lani and Suzanne were there, as well as a number of boys who were emerging as leaders. I took a seat near the end of the table, listening to their serious conversations peppered with emphatic gestures, Suzanne's hair bobbing as it always did as she spoke. There were a few empty seats near me, but the other tables were full. A white student approached my end of the table with a friend somewhere behind him.

"Are these seats taken?" he asked, and I nodded to him that they were empty. He sat down, and a few minutes later so did his friend. One of the boys at the other end began talking loudly.

"Do I see what I'm seeing?" he said. "Are there honkies sitting down at this table?"

A friend next to him took up his cue. "Yeah, I think I see some honkies sitting down there. In fact, I'm sure I see it. Some white butts filling those chairs."

Some people at the table began to laugh. It was a laugh that people have laughed since the beginning of time: the laugh of the ones with the upper hand. I stared at the two white students and tried to convey an apology with my eyes. I wanted to say that I was not laughing, that I was sorry, but the black boys at the other end of the table were staring as well, a look that was not lost on these boys. They both began to turn red in the face, then shuffled about in their seats, and then, finally apologizing, got up and left. When they did, uproarious laughter went up from part of the table.

It was after this lunch that I began to see the price of my easy admission. Like all groups, this one was going to extract its oath of loyalty. I had naively thought that I could combine the liberation of the people to whom I'd been born with the liberation of all people from the tyranny of prejudice and cruelty. But daily, there was the pressure to choose. Who you slept with, who you ate with, who you roomed with, what music you liked, all was subjected to this new scrutiny of loyalty to the race.

A few black people made the choice. If they wanted to have white friends, be a part of the larger white community in some fashion, they didn't participate in the black community. They had no black friends, went to no Afro meetings, and though they were laughed at occasionally, the confrontations were few. They gave up the ambivalence and slid off the edge of the black world. Others, like one of my roommates from a small town in Texas, had always moved exclusively in a black world and saw no reason to change. I, however, had cast a wider net, my loyalty based on shared values and ideals, not skin color. I was back to where I had begun at the beginning of the year, without an ideology that I knew how to defend. I took refuge in my supposed naiveté. To divert anger away from me, I played the fool. I pretended I didn't understand Black Power. I used the excuse that I always took things too personally. But all the while, I recalled the look on the black boys' faces when they slung their challenges to white boys: it was like those white people in Mount Vernon, smirking at each other when another white spoke in favor of busing. It was a look that was becoming more and more familiar to me.

Partly out of a desire to separate the two halves of my world, so that overlapping was rare, and partly because it was a smaller and more intimate environment, I began to spend most of my weekends at Brown. As an unknown in the university's black community, there were no tugs on my loyalty. Also, through my friend Brian I met a boy named Paul, a sweet and, I thought at first, somewhat shy black boy. I quickly learned however, that Paul wasn't shy. He had merely been absorbed in his own thoughts when we met, and once he turned his attention outward again, I discovered a kindred soul. He was tall and slender with beautiful hands and a dancer's body, and he was blessed with indefatigable energy and a hearty, deep laugh that rolled out of him. He was a marvel to everyone who got to know him. While others partied all night and slept through the day, Paul would dance until four in the morning, sleep for three hours, then get up, go to all of his classes, come back and study and read three newspapers, all before anyone else got up. He was a mixture of contrasts: he liked history and politics and dance. He was courtly and perversely ribald. He was as likely to know the name of the undersecretary of the interior as he was to know the second verse of a certain Gregorian chant. What we most liked to do together was talk and dance. On our dates we wandered from party to party, shouting at each other between songs until just before dawn. Then we would go back to his room and fall asleep in each other's arms.

With Paul I was able to be a black hippie. We wore bell-bottoms and beads, went to art installations down on the beach and concerts that went on for days. We listened to the Rolling Stones and the Grateful Dead, and with our white hippie friends were able to pretend that the future we were hoping for had already arrived. We also shared other experiences: like me, Paul had gone to a private high school, he was accustomed to the intimate tangle of friends that developed in those schools, he was from a comfortable suburban town, and he was more Southern than Northern in tempo and attitude, having been brought up in Virginia, just outside Washington. We were both at home in settings like these, where we got to know people as well as they knew themselves, where there was a kind of incestuousness to the relationships. Weekends were rounds of parties and discussions and events that wound and weaved among people and venues. We would start out in Brian's room, someone would suggest dinner, a small group would form and go off somewhere else, we would later regroup at a party, the party would spiral back to Brian's room.

Among our friends, the talk was always intense: the certainty we would find answers to all of the great questions that had puzzled humankind from the start, the absolute sureness that we were leaving outmoded distinctions behind. Race, class, even gender were to be washed away. It was a different kind of revolution from the black revolution, so entangled with issues of power and money. This one merely turned its back on the dominant culture, turned its back and built a new world, because it could. It was the world that I wanted to live in. Whereas I believed a black revolution would primarily benefit the many blacks who were economically and educationally oppressed, with this cultural revolution I believed I was creating the world I wanted to own.

Back at Radcliffe, I learned to make small accommodations that worked. I ignored the few people who bothered, after the first few months of policing, to make comments when I was seen with my white friends. I figured out which groups hung out where and when, so I could avoid certain confrontations. I went to meetings and signed petitions and went on strike from my classes, but I took a backseat role in Afro. I rarely spoke up at meetings. I was a loyal foot soldier with very little to say. I also picked and chose my friends. I roomed with soft-spoken Southern girls who may have disapproved of my friends and my music but were too polite to confront me, and whose rhythms I understood and could share. We could listen to the Edwin Hawkins Singers together, and I would turn on Jimi Hendrix when they were away.

Things would have continued this way — an uneasy truce between the real and the ideal — if two things hadn't happened. They were unrelated to politics, but they involved members of Afro, and as a result, they were again — illogically perhaps, but still inseparably — linked in my mind.

The first was a date I had with someone from Afro. Though Paul and I were still dating, it was an occasional thing. We had made no commitment to each other, so when this person asked me out, I said yes. He was one of the more vocal members of Afro, and a leader in the organization. He was just about my height, about my complexion, and a bit stockily built — not heavy, but not slim either — a muscled jock body. I had been introduced to him when a group of boys had come up to Radcliffe one night while we were playing cards. He was nice looking, and though not exactly soft-spoken, he wasn't the most talkative of the boys either. He acted a bit cool, but I thought that underneath he was probably nice. Perhaps I thought that dating him would be a way for me to feel more at ease within the larger black community at Harvard, that if I got to know people outside of those daunting political groups, that I would feel more at ease and could begin to express my opinions more confidently.

For our date we planned to go to a dance, one of the dozen or more mixers and dances and socials that went on at Harvard every weekend. My date suggested we meet at his room for a drink first. I remember he lived in a suite, as a lot of boys at Harvard did, but unlike others I'd been in, this suite had solid, adult furniture: a sofa and chairs that matched, even a table and some lamps. It looked like a grownup's room, not a student's. He made me a drink, a Scotch on the rocks. I took a few sips, and he took a few sips of his. He sat down next to me on the sofa, put his arm around me, and after a few minutes of talking, kissed me.

I was surprised, mainly because I wasn't even sure that he liked me. I had half suspected that he'd asked me out as a favor to Lani or Suzanne, with whom he shared Afro duties. Anyway, I didn't really want him to kiss me, because I didn't yet know him that well, but I didn't stop him. I remember thinking, A kiss, that's no big deal. It seemed like it would be more embarrassing to make a big deal out of it. Besides, maybe later I would want him to kiss me, and I didn't want to make him think he shouldn't maybe try again. So, he kissed and I let him, and as we kissed he began pushing me down on the couch. This was how I remembered his body so well, the feel of it unlike the bodies I'd felt so far — all of them more sinewy and rangy. I was a freshman and a virgin. Despite all the talk of free love, and a freedom I had never experienced before, I had done no more than hug and press against people I liked. I didn't believe I had to wait until I was married to have sex, but I knew I wasn't ready yet, and when I was, I knew I wanted it to be with someone I trusted and loved. This boy, however, was pushing at me in a way that no one had ever pushed at me before.

At first it almost didn't seem real. Why is he doing this? I thought. We hardly know each other and our date had barely begun.

At this point, he had me down and was on top of me, and he began not only kissing but moving his hands over my body. He was heavy, uncomfortably so, and clumsy, and hot, and I wanted none of it.

"Stop it," I said, "stop it." I moved my mouth away and turned my head, and to make my point very clear, I pushed at him with my hands. I tried to wriggle out from under him, and to my great surprise he kept on pushing. He noticed my resistance — I could feel him noting it and then deciding. He used his weight against me, used his muscle as well, and pushed. My arms he pinned down with his arms, my legs he pinned down with his legs. His body, the tenseness and anger, said to me plainly that there was no misunderstanding: he had registered what I said, knew what I was saying, and his reply was, So what, I am bigger and stronger than you.

As I felt him deciding to do what he would, a wave of humiliation washed over me. I felt my body go slack, giving in for the moment because I felt so stupid. I had never been treated this way by a boy before, and I lay there wondering how long it would take, if it would hurt, inert underneath him, as he started to unbutton my blouse. I could tell he had felt me go slack, and now he was set to begin. And just then, almost in spite of myself, I looked at him. I wanted to see the face that could treat me this way. He barely saw me. His face was flushed with excitement, he was beginning to breathe hard, and he wouldn't let his eyes settle on me. He was already past me, moving on his own to some point in the future that had nothing to do with me. And that was what finally aroused my anger: I was not even a specific object of desire, just an orifice. I made him look at me, twisting my head so that he could not avoid seeing my eyes.

"Get off of me," I said. He looked for a second, really annoyed, like he would do it now just to show me he could, and I looked back at him with all the fury I could muster, a cold fury. "Get off of me," I said even louder. For a long few moments I could see him weighing, considering. Would I scream? How hard would I fight? Would I tell anyone once it was over? I spoke back to him with my eyes. You do it, my eyes told him, and I will make your life a living hell. You will have to kill me after you do. I could still feel him weighing, considering. Whom would I tell? Would they believe me if I did? "Get off me!" I spat out again, and he pushed back against me, to hurt me, and then he got up.

"Stupid bitch," he said as I scrambled to my feet. He walked toward the kitchen area and then looked back at me and laughed. "Everyone said you were crazy," he told me. "I should have listened to them." When I left, as I did quickly, he was still chuckling under his breath.

Somehow his parting shot hurt me even more than the other: he revealed what I had just dimly, and I had hoped wrongly, suspected. I had spoken only a few times at Afro meetings. I felt awkward and upset much of the time. I didn't like a lot of the posturing. I didn't know how to pretend to be cool. I often felt, as I listened, that the utopia I sought to envision was gradually slipping away. But I had attributed most of this to my own nervousness. I believed that the intentions of everyone in the group were what they said they were, that it was only that I didn't know the right phrases and buzzwords. Surely my sincerity counted. Now I learned that I was not taken seriously. I was suffered as one suffers a fool.

I made my way back to my dorm. I didn't tell anyone — after all, what was there to tell? But then it happened again, in a slightly different way. I had met several boys through my friend Alta, one year my junior, but my soul mate in so many ways. She was as politically aware as Suzanne and Lani, but with her I could share my love of books and music and art. These young men she knew were also more into music and art, and we would sometimes hang out together, listening to music, discussing some burning topic of the day. They lived right near the Square, and sometimes when Alta and I walked by, one of them would yell out for us to come up and hear some new music.

One night one of these boys, a Harvard junior named Ted, called out and invited us up. When we got upstairs, we found that in addition to Ted there were four other boys in the room, boys whom Alta and I knew slightly. The room was dark and smoky, Ted's stereo was pounding out some jazz, and everyone, as usual, was talking at once. Introductions were made, we were offered some beer, and as we sat down, a discussion about the music, which we'd obviously just interrupted, resumed.

I leaned forward in my chair, hoping to follow what was being said, but since I didn't recognize the music and was not that well versed in jazz, I eventually gave up. People floated in and out of the room, the music got louder, every once in a while someone laughed.

At some point I began to feel uncomfortable. I attributed it, at first, to the fact that I didn't know these people well and didn't know anything about the topic at hand. I sat back in my oversized chair and drank my beer. I tried to take my cues from Alta, who after all knew these boys better than I did. From what I could tell, she seemed at ease. Yet each time I came back to the mood in the room, I sensed a rhythm, an energy that I didn't like.

I kept looking at Alta to see if she was noticing what I felt, but she was laughing, leaning back in her chair, her feet up on a table. Relax, Parker, I tried to tell myself, relax. This is why you have such a hard time with people. You just don't know how to relax. At some point Alta got up to go to the bathroom. There was an almost electric charge in the room, but white-hot, aggressive, not warm. I began to feel that the laughter was directed at us. Maybe I am just being paranoid, I thought.

One of the guys talking to Ted laughed again. He looked at me and then over to Alta, who was coming back into the room.

It was a look that I'd seen before. Impersonal, predatory.

"We can run a train on them," this boy said. A couple of the other boys nodded, also looking our way.

I sat upright in my seat. I had heard this expression. Run a train. I knew what it meant. A bunch of guys, one girl or two. Each of them takes her in turn.

I thought I was hearing things. "You want to?" someone else asked.

"Yeah, man, easy." Someone else laughed. "They are so out of it. We can easily get it over on them."

I grabbed Alta's arm as she made for her chair. "Come here," I said, "come here." She followed me off to another part of the room. "They are talking about raping us," I said.

"What?" she asked, her eyes shining brightly. I could tell she was high with the music and the beer.

"They said they are going to run a train on us," I said. "We've got to go, we've got to go."

I didn't know if Alta believed me. Perhaps she thought I was making it up. But my upset, she could tell, was real, as was my fear.

"OK," she said, "we can go," though I could feel her reluctance.

I kept a tight grip on her arm as we hurriedly collected our things and said our goodbyes.

"Why do you have to rush off?" Ted asked, and for a moment I wondered if I had imagined the whole thing. But then I replayed the look in that first boy's eyes, and I looked at him now, and saw it again. I pulled Alta alongside me as we nearly ran down the steep flight of stairs to the street. As soon as we left, the room erupted in laughter.

I later realized that the boys probably hadn't really been talking about rape. If they had, given their number, they could easily have stopped us from going. But the aggression was nonetheless real. It was harsh and ugly and self-centered, and it took our ease and our comfort and our trust, which was stupid and a little naive, and flung it back in our faces. And that was what had hurt — that we should have been cast out, yet again I thought, from the possibility of real community.

After those two incidents with men who wanted me to call them my brothers, I was never able to look at the political side of the Black Power movement in the same way. Clearly, there was a whole side of black people, namely the female side, that was being given short shrift by the movement. All the talk of freedom and unity and respect began to have a hollow ring. Whose freedom? I asked myself. United to do what? Respect from whom and for what? My close brush with date rape, my supposed friends talking about running a train, even the off-hand jokes that some boys had made about real rape — making babies for the revolution, they called it — I saw these images whenever someone in Afro spoke about freedom. It made me wonder exactly how far such talk of freedom would go.

I had always been suspicious of groups. Before coming to Radcliffe, I had shied away from groups: there was a dynamic there that often alarmed me. I associated them with mindlessness, with pettiness, even with cruelty. It had been a group of girls, after all, that had sought to beat me up in grammar school. It had been groups of people that had yelled racial epithets in Mount Vernon, egging each other on. It was always within the safety of small, tight groups that kids at the Jack and Jill dances made snide comments about others who were not cool enough, not light enough in complexion. Now, whenever I went to Afro meetings and saw the boys scrambling to claim power over the girls, or even recalled the gleeful venom that was sometimes heaped upon whites, it made me wonder if these excesses were not always where the pursuit of power for its own sake, unfettered by a larger principle, would lead. I kept attending the meetings, took part in the demonstrations, felt committed to many of the group's goals, but I felt ensnared in this double vision. I could not wholeheartedly embrace the group and its aims. As I watched people jockey for position, I asked myself: If we were installed in power the next day, would we be any different or better than the group we sought to unseat?

During my sophomore and junior years in college I took several trips to the South. The first one was back to North Carolina with some of my Radcliffe friends, to attend a black student conference in Durham. The trip, for me, was fraught with expectations. I had never ventured beyond the Harvard-Radcliffe environs with any of my new friends. Lani, Suzanne, a roommate of mine from Texas named Loretta, Alta, and I traveled together, and with the exception of Alta we were all going to stay at my grandmother McDougald's house. I wanted to be a gracious hostess, I wanted everyone to be comfortable, and I particularly hoped to show off my hometown and the black community I was familiar with. I had never been able to find the words to express what I felt at Afro meetings — the dissatisfactions, the desire to expand the definition of who we were as a people — and, in my mind, this trip was a way of easing some of these tensions. It was a bid for dialogue that was going to be shaped without words.

Our first stop en route was my parents' house in Mount Vernon. I was proud of my parents: my father was his usual outgoing and talkative self, my mother was warm and welcoming. Their careers kept them in touch with the political and social upheavals of the day, and my father was amused by and willing to debate some of our more radical ideas. We laughed, talked, had a huge meal, and everything was just right: down-home, not pretentious, my parents not afraid to use the new word "black," not daunted by our huge afros. I felt as if the alchemy I hoped to effect with the trip was already under way.

This feeling continued all the way to Durham, where we stopped at a small restaurant when we got into town. It was a home-cooking kind of place, and I bantered easily with the waitress. A few customers recognized me and we exchanged warm greetings. I knew what was good on the menu, steered my friends to the best items, and lapsed into the cadences of speech that I had thought were long forgotten. It was as if my past were a good-looking man with whom I was flirting, and with every gesture I was inviting him closer to me. Loretta quickly joined in the banter, and for a few minutes we were like two local guides, eagerly and proudly showing off what the Southern corner of the world had to offer.

The next morning, at my grandmother's house, we all gathered in the large kitchen. It was a Saturday, so Lucille wasn't there, and my grandmother took her time upstairs, I think trying to stay out of our way as best she could. My friends and I bustled about the kitchen, pulling together a big Southern breakfast. As always, the morning sunlight cascaded into the room, just as it used to when I would go over to my grandmother's house for a second breakfast as a child. Outside the window I could see all that was so familiar to me: our old house across the expanse of the back yard, Cousin R.C. and Knotsie's house, Cousin Pearl and Ulysses's house, and the college across Lawson, which had expanded far up the hill and into what had been an empty lot down the street. And I looked at my friends, who were, as I and my grandmother had so strenuously urged, making themselves to home. We were laughing and teasing one another, and I saw us as we might have appeared from the outside: Suzanne, her red hair awry, every move across the kitchen in her favorite Dr. Scholl's sandals an emphatic, audible snap; Lani, almost regal, even in her nightshirt, ever the conciliatory presence; me, a little puppy-doggish and eager to please; and Loretta, with her womanly figure, reserved and held deeply within herself. All of us black, all of us bright, our shades of color spanning all hues. I wondered, as I had wondered so many times before, what united us, what separated us. We called ourselves sisters, but what did that mean?

Suddenly, under the weight of my thoughts, we all seemed to break apart, splinter into distinct parts. I saw each of us as composed of not just this moment but of all the moments that had come before, and not only that, but all of the meanings that had come before. We imagined a shared history, but the weight of my own personal one revealed that to be an illusion. My grandmother was a conservative, small-town woman to whom manners and taste mattered. Lani's maternal grand-mother had been Jewish, Suzanne's maternal grandmother Italian — what would these three women have had in common? And would my friends' grandmothers' homes have contained the same smells? Would breakfast have assumed the same importance? Had Lani and Suzanne even spent time with their grandmothers, and if they had, how did their memories of that time shape their internal landscape? And what was Loretta's grandmother's home like? It was clear to me that despite outward appearances, we had each been shaped by thousands of moments that made us fundamentally different from one another. My perspective would always be molded by the fact of the black college across the street from me, by the fact of the neighbors and relatives behind me, by the sunny brick house filled with books that my grandfather's money had built, and by the countless other moments that were part of my particular experience. The black that we each wore was woven of these myriad strands, some overlapping, some totally incompatible with the others' version of black.

I had hoped to form a new community without words, but I now knew that this silent dialogue was not going to be nearly enough, that we would have to sit down at that breakfast table and begin to acknowledge the gulfs that lay between us and to see what common ground we shared.

But at the time, I did not have the courage to say all this, and merely standing in that place wasn't an adequate substitute. I had shown my friends all that had once been so familiar to me, what had once been the definition of the world itself, and I felt it break apart under the weight of its particularity. This was not *the* world, I now saw, just my own version of it. *The* world, a common one, was still waiting. We drove back up north, our respective versions of black still unexplored terrain.

During my junior year, much to my surprise and dismay, I got pregnant. Paul and I had dated throughout our college years, and it was nearly two years before we had gone any further than kissing. Though it was an admittedly illogical train of thought, I was almost angry at the turn of events: it seemed a harsh punishment for only one night of inattention, and it didn't seem fair. I had waited so much longer than most of the girls I knew, and still the thing I had been warned about had happened right away. I had thought that surely there would be some kind of grace period for sex, as if it would take my body a while to get to know what it was doing. But it knew long before I did, and my irregular period meant that by the time I found out, a deadline for a decision was at hand.

From the start, I knew what I would probably do. There was never any real doubt in my head, even though Paul valiantly offered to marry me, and we even went so far as to tell all of our friends we were engaged. But it was play-acting, and I knew it. I was no more ready to be a mother and wife than Paul was ready to be a husband and father. When I went home for Christmas, I knew I would have to somehow tell my parents.

It was the first time I had ever contravened, in any major way, the rules that my parents had set out for my life. I had never acted contrary to the script I'd been given. I was a good student, I was in a good school, I was respectful to my elders, and even now, even as I skipped classes and stayed out late to party, I always drew the line. So when the time came to study for tests, I would do it. I would go around and get the notes from people who had been to class. I would pull all-nighters for weeks on end and get the grades I needed to stay in school and do well. I was not one of those students who took the freedom and the rebellion and pushed them too far — the ones who flunked out or took too many drugs and ended up in the hospital, who crossed the dividing line and couldn't get back. At bottom, I knew where I'd come from, and what that said about where I was going, and all the hippie free love wasn't going to change that. And I knew that was true as well for Paul.

We weren't going to drop out, he wasn't going to leave Brown and go to night school, I wasn't going to take a job to support us during the day — these just weren't among the options. We knew what we had to do. The only thing was, how would I tell my parents?

I remembered scant conversations with my parents about sex. My mother told me the facts of life when I was ten. She accompanied it with a booklet and a package of Tampax so I would be ready. In my late teens, my father said something to me about how boys sometimes liked to try things, and you had to be careful, but that was all I remembered. Now, this looming conversation was the most embarrassing thing I could think of — to tell my parents what I had done, what had happened, and most of all, to feel that I had let them down.

All Christmas I could think of nothing else. My clothes were already tight at the waist, and I tried a hundred times to bring up the subject, but each time my nerve failed me. Yet I couldn't go back to school without telling them. Abortions had just been made legal in New York, but I couldn't even think of going through it alone.

I still hadn't said anything to my parents by the end of vacation. They left for work on the day I was to return to Cambridge, and I lay on their bed and cried. At some point the phone rang, and it was my mother. She was calling to remind me about something, I don't remember what, and I just blurted it out.

"I'm pregnant," I said.

"I will call your father," she said.

My father called a few minutes later. "Are you all right?" he asked. I was sobbing and hiccupping and nearly unable to talk.

"We are not happy," he said, "but this isn't the end of the world. Your mother and I will be home soon."

An hour or so later, my parents came home. I was still sitting where I'd been when they phoned, at the head of their bed, when I heard the door open downstairs. I thought about getting up, but my legs were too shaky. I was terrified of what they would do and say. I saw their heads appear over the banister as they walked upstairs, and I tried to read their faces. But I was too scared. I was twenty years old, but I was a child and these were my parents, awesome and huge. My mother came into the room first, and she held her arms out to me. I stood up and nearly fell into them, and she hugged me tightly to her. When she was through, my father took her place, each of them holding me up so I wouldn't fall to the floor. I was crying and crying and neither of them seemed to mind. It had been a long time since hugs comforted so, since my parents hugged me the way they had when I was little.

I don't think I have ever felt as loved by my parents as I did that day, and felt as glad to be black. Perhaps being black had nothing to do with it, perhaps I was deluded, but all of the stories I had heard of parents throwing their children out on the street, of mothers or fathers calling their children names, had been about white families. My parents came home and hugged me, it was the first thing they both did. I don't remember all that was said, but I do remember their arms around me. They were upset, this was a problem that had to be dealt with, but I was their daughter and they loved me and I was not about to be cast out. This is blackness, I kept thinking, loving without reserve and without judgment. It took me all the way back to the beginning, to that feeling of a place that had once welcomed me and taken me in. I wanted to run back to school and tell everyone at Afro that this was what Black Power should be about, this was indeed the feeling upon which any and all movements should be based. My parents were not perfect by any means, but for me they were perfect that day.

Later, after the abortion was all over, Paul drove to Mount Vernon to pick me up and take me back to school. He had volunteered to do this. We had talked over the phone for hours, and he kept saying he should face my parents — it wasn't fair that I should go through all this alone. He had met my parents several times before, and they liked him. I told my father that Paul was coming, and my father said that he was glad to hear it, that he wanted to talk to him. When Paul pulled up in his car, I went out to the curb and saw him sitting there for a moment, composing himself.

"What do you think he's going to say?" he asked as we walked toward the house.

"I don't know," I said, but I was scared, as much for Paul as for myself. I worried that my father might yell at him, as he had sometimes yelled at me as a child, and I wondered if Paul would dissolve into tears as I usually did.

We went inside and my mother greeted Paul with a hug and kiss. My father shook his hand and took him into the kitchen. My mother and I sat in the living room while the two men talked. There was no screaming, no pounding on the table. When Paul came out, he was still in one piece. We stayed for a few hours, had a little something to eat, talked about school and classes and future plans, and then were on our way.

"What did he say?" I asked Paul as soon as we got into his car.

Paul shook his head, as if he still couldn't believe that he had survived the visit. "He said that a lot of men think that they should just go as far as they can, and that it's up to the girl to say no. But he said he didn't agree with that. He believed it was both the boy's and the girl's responsibility to do what was careful, up to both of us to say no. Neither of us was bad, he said, but we had both acted irresponsibly."

I marveled at this, along with Paul, and was deeply grateful. I had always looked up to my parents. Now I felt there were things about them that I was just beginning to learn.

My hippie life and my black revolutionary life were like two opposing legs that I stood on at college. Rarely were they traveling in the same direction. Being a hippie took me toward art and music and a free-floating experience that had little to do with responsibility. Being a black revolutionary meant being constantly serious and feeling responsible for my whole race. As a hippie, I acted in plays, went to parties that lasted all weekend, sat up nights feverishly devouring novels and plays and poetry, wore clothes that looked as if they came from a carnival. As a black revolutionary, I read treatises and tomes, debated tactics and methods of dissent, occupied buildings and went on strike from my classes.

What I most desperately wanted and could not find was a way to bring the two sides of myself into some kind of balance, to get them walking along a single path that would make sense for me. But I found no way to thread the disparate strains of my life into anything even closely resembling a unified being. Most of all, there was no group with whom I could stand and say, Here is where I belong. My white hippie friends could plan now for a life that did not have to admit, as mine did, the existence of grave imperfections in society. They could make their own little world, or live among racists, and simply not know. My black revolutionary friends could fashion a statement of principle based on the evil of white oppression, and that alone would form their yardstick of meaning. If white people were left out, so much the better. The questions I brought to each group were not ones that they were at all inclined to answer.

As senior year approached, all the play-acting of the previous years began to fall away. Whatever new personas my classmates had tried on, old ones reasserted themselves. Doctors' sons applied to medical school. Lawyers' daughters took the LSAT. As for me, panic set in. I began to genuinely fear that I was not the daughter my family wanted. Up until then, with only occasional lapses, I had met all of their expectations. Now it seemed that we argued all the time, about what I was interested in, about what I would be. I raised the idea of writing or acting, but neither met with any enthusiasm from my family.

All of us at Harvard and Radcliffe were expected to do something great. According to the myth of the place, we were all destined to be leaders — that was why we were chosen and that was the destiny we had to fulfill. For us blacks it was no different; in fact, the burden was even more heavy. We were pulling the entire race along with us. Who would open the doors if not us? Who would break down the barriers if we didn't? We were carrying not just ourselves but our ancestors too. My grandmother Parker raised the specter of her father, of his rise from slavery, of his life of toil and upward progression, again and again. My mother's ancestors and their lofty achievements were silent reminders too. And everywhere people were sorting themselves out, making plans, pulling on the cloaks of destiny and responsibility. I looked around and could find no role models to follow.

I didn't flunk out, I kept my grades up, but I was slipping, directionless. None of the parts up to now would cohere. I was a Southern black middle-class girl primed for success. I was too much affected by feelings. I loved writing and acting and staring into space and watching everything go by. I was my parents' bright and obedient girl. Most of all, I was desperate for a way to belong to the world in a way that felt both relevant and soulful. What would I do with my dreams of inclusion if I chose to live in a segregated world? What would I do with my parents' and my community's dreams if I turned my back on success? How would I live at all if I followed my own path, which at that time seemed impossibly murky?

Eventually I gave up on reason and began to live on impulse. I grew proficient at making decisions that looked like decisions but weren't decisions at all. In the winter of my senior year, Paul and Brian applied to take the LSAT, since they both intended to become lawyers. I had nothing to do that Saturday, so without any preparation I signed up for and took the LSAT too. At the same time, I began to notice all of the older students who haunted Harvard Yard, in graduate school, getting their Ph.D.s in something or other, who seemed caught in half a life — too old to still be students, too enamored of student life to go out and get a real job. Fearing that as my future, I decided I would not stay at Harvard, and I would not go to another university town. Instead, I would go where the real world was. And what could be more real than

New York? So that was where I decided to go. With each step I took, other decisions were made, all wholly random, unfolding as if there were an established plan when there was no plan at all. Graduation approached. What are your plans? my father asked me.

The only things I was sure I knew how to do were study and get decent grades. That I had not emerged as a leader, or with a sure sense of mission or career, made me feel all the more unsure of myself. All the while, my parents reminded me of the privileges I'd had, of the opportunities available to someone like me. I felt blessed and lucky, as I always had, but these blessings carried responsibilities equally as weighty. The ancestral voices were rumbling. I had been gifted with a brain, I had always been told. I was an excellent student. I could become a lawyer easily, and from there, who knew where my career would end? I would become a professional, as all in my family were, but one rung higher. I would be able to make a decent living, have a good life. Most important, I would not drop out, leaving a seat empty for a white person to fill.

The obvious route seemed to stare me in the face. Weren't there two good law schools, Columbia and New York University, right in New York City? Hadn't I already taken the LSAT and done well? Didn't all of these things mean that a lawyer was what I was meant to be?

So I leapt. I quizzed Suzanne and her roommate, who were both in law school, on the merits of each school, decided on NYU, and presented myself at the admissions office sometime in the late summer of 1973.

The secretary in the office laughed at me. They had thousands of applicants, she told me, the sorting was almost over, letters of acceptance had already gone out — surely I didn't think I could jump right in, at this late date. But I knew about the search for qualified black students — "qualified" being a code word for "just like all the other students we have ever accepted" — and where would they find a student more like the ones they were used to than me? We were a mere handful, because of the generations of whites who had kept the doors closed to so many — but a handful nevertheless, and I knew this.

"I would like to speak to the dean," I said. I made such a commotion that the dean must have heard me from inside his office, and he came out.

"I would like to apply for this fall," I said. "I know it is late, but I graduated from Radcliffe with good grades, I did well on my LSAT, and I am not looking for a scholarship."

"Give her an application," the dean said.

Thus began my legal career. A last-minute decision, a last-minute appeal for entry. It was not something I had dreamed about as a child. It was not something I had a burning desire to do. In fact, beyond lawyer, the word itself, I couldn't say what it was I expected. What I did know was that it was a graduate school, and only three years, with a test at the end. It would give me a job, and more than that, a career. I didn't know who I should be, or how to achieve it if I'd been able to name it. So I would be my parents' and my grandparents' progeny. If nothing else, that was something I knew how to do.

FIVE

The Letter of the Law

I N MY FIRST WEEK AT NYU, the law school newspaper printed on its front page the average LSAT scores of the incoming black students and compared them to the average white students' scores. The spread between the two was considerable: for whites the average was somewhere in the 600s, for blacks the low 500s to the high 400s (on a scale that ranged from 200 to 800). As one of the top law schools, NYU was of course concerned with attracting the best and the brightest students, and scores in the 600s were considered excellent. The 500s, though not as laudable, were still respectable.

I later learned that the school had for several years printed the average LSAT scores of the incoming students, but this was the first time the scores had been broken down by race or ethnicity. The article was not long, but the implications were clear: as a group, we black students were attending NYU under special circumstances (in fact, there was a screening process for minorities at the time, a so-called special admissions process, resulting in a group called "special admittees"); we did not meet the otherwise rigorous standards set by the school; and other students, arguably more qualified white students, had been displaced in order to admit us. (The same argument was made several years earlier by a white applicant named Defunis, whose case was dismissed by the Supreme Court as moot in the spring of my first year at law school, because by then Defunis would already have graduated from the school that the trial court had ordered he be allowed to enter.)

The newspaper article was only one among several that touched on the notion of a special admissions process for minorities. The subject itself pitted several arguments against each other. One was that lawyers were professionals trained to serve the needs of their communities. In order to serve every community, then, the law school should have a representative mix of students. This argument was one to which some of the faculty subscribed. A second argument regarded law school, and its gatekeeping role, as the passage to a certain life and standard of living, as a plum that should be awarded only to those who, as evidenced by scores and grades, had bested their peers. This was the view that, at least among the students I talked with, appeared to be most commonly held. A final argument was a variation on the second one: while not challenging the notion of rewards based on some meritocratic ranking, it merely stated that minorities required additional, or different, measures of merit.

My reaction to the article was hardly dispassionate. I was at first shocked that such a disclosure had been made, and then deeply embarrassed. The subject opened up, for me, an age-old wound: the charge that intellectually, as a race, we did not measure up. Moreover, the disclosure of the scores felt ugly and mean-spirited, because while the professors may have rationally debated social policy, we students were the ones clamoring for our places at the starting gate. The disclosure was presented with a veneer of objective information, yet I could feel immediately what I was sure was its real intended effect — namely, to trip a few of us up and, when we faltered, shoulder us out of the way. We could not now be turned back — we were already here — but the coming competition was a race that would be determined as much by self-confidence as it would be by skill. Just as we were set to dash out of the gate, we were all of us, as blacks, deprived of a reliable competitive aid.

Though law school had never been a long-sought goal for me, there was no denying its social currency. For every student, whether it was a lifelong dream or merely following in Daddy's footsteps, the feeling of arrival was palpable as we all went about the routines of registration and orientation. We were on the verge of transformation from college students to professionals — people who, from here on out, wherever we went, would be able to command at least a grudging respect from society.

None of us was immune to the feeling — almost despite myself, I felt it as well — so when that article appeared, the effect on the black students was almost physically apparent. Smiles hardly cocky to begin with were wiped off of our faces. Our steps were no longer as sure. Whereas others had earned their places here, our coinage, we were told, was counterfeit.

My response quickly turned from embarrassment to anger. I wanted to find out which editor had decided this would make a good opening-week story, which writer had written it, the people who'd concurred with the decision to run it, and then I wanted to expose their own vulnerabilities — everyone must have something to hide, I figured. But I had to remind myself that this was not what I was here for, and I threw myself into the heavy workload and tried to forget about the article.

I thought I had succeeded in putting it out of my mind, until several days later, when I was studying in the library. I was sitting in a small, nearly empty room that adjoined the main room, reading and taking notes on cases, when a white student approached me. I don't remember if he had been sitting in the room studying as well or had just come in, all I remember is that he was suddenly at my table, speaking to me as if he were resuming a conversation that had been interrupted.

"A lot of us are kind of mad," he said. I looked up when I heard his voice, mainly to see to whom he might have been speaking. I was surprised that he appeared to be talking to me.

"What?" I asked. His face had a serious expression, and he was rubbing his hands on the table nervously.

"You know, the article in the paper a few days ago. A lot of us are pretty upset."

"Us?" I asked.

"We white students."

"White students?" I asked. I was still confused. I briefly wondered if he was part of some organization or was taking a survey of which I was unaware. I felt as if my attention had lapsed in the middle of a movie. Surely there was an explanation for why this stranger was talking to me.

I imagine the look on my face told him that I didn't have the slightest idea what he was talking about. "The article in the *paper*," he repeated. "About the *scores*."

Now I understood him. With his cozy "us," he had sneaked up on my hard-sought solitude like some sort of racial grenade and neatly riven the world in two.

I pushed my chair a little way back from the table. I wished that there were other black students in the room to whom I could appeal, or that I were bigger and heavier, more intimidating somehow. But I was alone, an easy and unthreatening target, female and approachable.

I was always taken aback by encounters with the type of white people who assumed they had access to me which was wholly unearned. These people were like children who approach any reputable-looking adult, secure that their needs will be met. But still it surprised me. I tried to imagine myself going up to a white person I didn't know and starting a conversation in this way, and it was unimaginable. I looked at this student again and could see his growing agitation. This was far from an academic question to him.

"You think you're smarter than the other black students, is that what you're saying?" I asked.

"That's what the whole thing's about," he answered, as if I were being purposely dense.

A parade of white people marched through my mind, all of them with their mouths tightly pursed around words like "standards" and "measuring up." I wanted to take a thick stick and mow them all down. That isn't what it's about by a long shot, I wanted to scream at this student. But I held out a glimmer of hope. After all, this was law school, where, presumably, logic was held in the highest esteem. Maybe I could educate him on matters of advantage and privilege.

"You can't really say that," I said. "It's like a race. Suppose, at the gun, some people start out sprinting and others have their feet tied together for the first half of the competition. Then, just before the finish line, those whose feet are bound are suddenly set free. You can't just look at the end of the race,"

I explained. "You have to see whether it was fair all along."

But as I spoke, I could see incomprehension in his eyes. In his world only the present existed, only the scores and what they said about absolute worth. I grew angry again at the willful narrowness of this view. And then I realized that it must have been fate that had chosen me as this white person's particular target. I heard my grandmother Parker's voice, my father's, the voices of everyone who had ever encouraged me in this intellectual gambit, for reasons often unfathomable to me. They were beside me now, urging me on. I felt as if this brain I'd been blessed with had been given to me for this moment alone. If my abilities were good for nothing else, they were good for this.

"OK," I said, warming to my new role, "let's just use the two of us as an example. Let's let the two of us be representative of our races. How does that sound to you?"

"Fine," he said, obviously pleased that I was finally going in the direction that he felt was right from the start.

"OK," I said, "let's start with schools. Where did you go to undergraduate school?"

He named a perfectly respectable state university in the Midwest.

"OK," I said, as if I were ticking off points on a tally. "I went to Harvard. So in terms of schools, mine was better, wouldn't you say?"

He nodded, but he didn't look so sure of himself.

"Now, how about grades. What was your grade point average?"

He told me, and I beat him there by a few tenths of a point.

"OK, now on to the LSAT," I said. "That was what the whole article was about, right?"

"Right," he answered, still confident that it would all come out in the end.

"Right," I said. "Now, what was your score?"

He said it with neither pride nor apology but with faith. He was representative, his voice said, surely I would be as well. His score was in the high 500s, below the average score for whites admitted to the school, but still far above the average score for the blacks.

My score was, on the other hand, in the range of the average white score for the school. I said the number quickly, tossing it off. In the world of the LSAT, even ten points could represent thousands of students. These students, legions of them, now popped up between us to form an impassable wall, separating my performance from his.

He looked stunned. That I might have lied never occurred to either of us, and he continued to stare at me, as if hoping for some further explanation.

"So, just between the two of us," I went on, "I'd say you were pretty lucky to be here, wouldn't you say?"

I made a slow show of gathering my books and papers, and then I left him standing there, demolished. When, as a child, I'd schemed to make my teachers look stupid, there had been an innocence about it, but now my innocence was gone. I savored the look I left on that man's face, a look of not only defeat but disarray, as if something had been undone in his world that could never be made right again. It was infinitely more satisfying than using my fists. It was such a small and cheap victory, but I hugged it tightly to my chest.

From that first encounter with the white student, I had found my place in the school, that of racial avenger. It was a lonely role. There were no comrades to share in my fight, as it was always a singular contest between me and one other student, invariably a white male. The rules of the game were as follows: I would never initiate the battle, I even tried to remain aloof from it, but when challenged, I would fight to the end. The end was the look in the eye that said, My God, this black woman is as smart, if not smarter, than I am. I didn't want to be more interesting, sweeter, more competitive, more aggressive, I wanted the playing field level in this one area alone: intellectual ability. Whose mind was sharper, more facile, able to penetrate deeper and faster — this was the thing that white males clung to as their natural advantage, and it was the only thing that I wanted to wrest from them. It became my passion.

Law school, of course, was the natural arena for playing this game. In many professions, one attribute is singled out above others, and in law school being smart was all, with "smart" being narrowly defined as an ability to poke holes in others' arguments, to demolish your opponent's position. If my grandmother Parker believed that being smart was a valuable asset, in law school it was the only asset — all other attributes were subsumed under this one pointy goal. To instill this value, professors at New York University used the so-called Socratic method of teaching. In practice, to me this meant that the professors set out to browbeat and humiliate the students in order to arouse their aggressive and competitive instincts.

There were two black professors when I was at NYU, and one of them made the mistake of trying to be kind to the students. He was young, and perhaps he remembered too vividly how it had felt to be in law school and vowed to make it different. Whatever the reason, he was gentle with his charges.

He took great pains not to belittle people. He tried to get them to see the errors of their thinking without the usual haughtiness that the other professors assumed. He did not laugh at people or snort in disbelief when someone's remarks went far afield. He was much more approachable than the other professors, always willing to stay after class to explain things to students with questions. This turned out to be a grave miscalculation on his part. He assumed his intellectual stature was a given, but in this world, a black professor had to prove it.

I learned this from the other black professor, who took the offensive right from the start. He was brilliant and haughty and as hard, if not harder, on students as the other professors. He had perfected a certain laugh, barely a half laugh, as if he wouldn't waste energy on your ignorance, and he used it whenever a student was heading down the wrong path of an argument. The laugh would start in his eyes and creep slowly down to his lips. After class, he had no more than a minute or two to spare. Go back and read the cases, he'd say, and then that laugh again.

Perhaps this professor recognized in me a kindred racial warrior, because he seemed to be as drawn to me as I was to him. His was the only course in which I had a personal interest. I studied harder for his class than I did for any other, determined to give him the gift of my supreme effort, of my pure, unadulterated respect. In my second year I became this professor's research assistant. Later, when we had become friends, I asked him why he was so hard on his students, harder even than the white professors were.

"If I don't make them look like fools, every one of them," he said, "they will not give me their respect. It's a horrible system, but that's how it works. A white professor can afford to be nice. They will accept that from him, but not from me."

I learned well from my mentor. If my experiences in Mount Vernon had not proved it to me, law school certainly did: I had a killer instinct when it came to intellectual matters, and like my mentor, I rose to the challenge. However, there was a key caveat to my game: except in my mentor's class, I purposefully put forward less than a full effort. Striving to be the absolute best would have meant validating the ruthlessly competitive game we were playing, and I didn't want to win at that particular game. I simply wanted to keep my color in their face. Along the way, I saw that I had a facility for law, just as my family had always predicted.

But beyond my private war, there was little of the racial politics that had been so prominent at Harvard. Here, people just lacked the time. Instead, they began sorting themselves into groups based on their perceptions of where they might fall in the class. The better students sought out the other better students to study with; the ones who were floundering looked for others like themselves to pore over cases with at night. Some black students, like me, managed to stay afloat; too many others couldn't keep up the pace, their spirits crushed daily by the assumptions, among many of their classmates and professors, of their deficiencies, which they could no longer deflect.

By the spring of my second year, another sorting out began: the law-firm interviews. There was no on-campus recruiting for first-year students, so our class had to wait until its second year to participate in this annual ritual. Unlike a lot of other prestigious law schools, NYU did not publish or create a class ranking, but the law school journals selected their staffs from the top portion of the class, and so the best students could proudly display that honor on their résumés. It was from this invisible ranking that the law firms were able to choose who it was they might wish to interview for positions as summer associates with their firms. Everyone knew who these lucky few were, because they suddenly started wearing suits to school.

Among the chosen, there appeared to be only two black students: me and another black woman. For the two weeks or so that recruiting went on, it was as if all of us at the top had been knighted. Other students subtly moved out of our way or held open doors for us, and the suits sailed through. Suits began talking mainly to other suits. If a suit in a group of students said something about a case, all of the others stopped to listen. Suits could interrupt others without incurring disfavor. And having tasted this first victory, having won in this first official sorting out, we suits were now predisposed toward believing that things would always go our way, that we would forever be insulated from failure.

The real prize in all of this was very clear: the jobs that paid the most money. The summer before law school, as a substitute teacher, I had been paid $30 a day. My mother, as a full-time high school dean in Mount Vernon, after twenty years in her field, earned less than $12,000 a year. As summer associates, we were to be paid in the neighborhood of $8,000, at that time a staggering sum. I had never considered what kind of work I would do as a lawyer. It had never entered my thoughts. But here I was, being courted by firms that were going to pay me more in a summer than I had ever earned in a year. The lure was irresistible. Besides, I thought, Why not? What's the harm? So I put on my suit, went to my interviews, brought out my best boarding school charm, tempered now with the self-confidence of knowing I was among the best, and waited to see if I would be offered a prize, a coveted summer associate's job.

Before one interview, I was approached by another suit in the student lounge. Without any preliminaries, he came up to me and bemoaned the advantage he believed I had. "You are going to have your pick of the jobs. Female and black. Everybody is going to want you," he said. "I'll be lucky if I get even one offer. It just isn't fair."

I had to admit that his notion of fairness was interesting. That all of his life he had had advantages that others would yearn for was lost on him. "It's not my fault that white males at the top of the class are a dime a dozen," I said, though I knew I was not making a dent in his world-view.

I received two or three job offers and decided to accept one from an old white-shoe firm in New York, Cadwalader, Wickersham & Taft. I can remember neither my other offers nor what in particular made me choose Cadwalader. It may have been the interviewer. Cadwalader's main recruiting partner at the time had a way of putting the students at ease. He reminded me, in fact, of many preppies I'd known: jocular, smooth, handsome in a Waspy way. I thought I could handle a firm filled with adult versions of the Taylors and Morgans and Dicks I had gone to school with. Of course, once I got there, I would learn that guys like this were the Trojan horses, handpicked for their ability to sucker us students in.

If I were male, I would describe a summer associate at a major law firm as the equivalent of a businessman in a bar who doesn't realize he's being hustled by a whore even when he's told to pay up. I'm not sure if there is a female analogy — not that we don't have our pride, only that we are so rarely hustled by it. At any rate, whatever the gender genesis of the game, it was one that worked exceedingly well. It worked because, like most people, I was vulnerable to flattery and fawning. It worked because it was a heady feeling to suddenly be told that you are one of the best.

We summer associates worked hard, but the assignments were carefully picked to be interesting, the partners were on their best behavior, and the whole summer was a nearly endless round of parties and the ostentatious display of the lifestyle that would one day be ours if we would only say yes. There was a boating afternoon at someone's country club in Rye, all dark green trees and blue waves, with lots of fruity drinks by the pool; there was the barbecue and evening party out at a partner's enormous house in New Jersey; there were formal outings at places like the Union Club, and lunches at steak houses with thousand-dollar leather chairs, and dinners at French restaurants that ended with flambéed desserts. We were feted and courted and seduced.

When the summer was over, I went back to my third year of law school with an offer of a full-time job in hand. As other students pored over books in the placement office and worried about whether a job offer would come, all I had to do was say yes and show up in the fall. When I told my parents about the position I'd been offered, they acted as if there were nothing to discuss. It was the top, what else needed to be said? After all, it was what I'd been groomed for. My grandmother Parker was particularly proud. I would be opening so many doors, she told me. As a Wall Street attorney, I would be going where few of my race had gone.

I pretended to make a decision, but in reality, the decision was already made. I could no more refuse this opportunity than I could cease to be the person I was. During college, as a member of the revolution and Woodstock Nation, I had shunned Wall Street and railed against big business and whoever supported it as corrupt and greedy and evil, but being one of the best was the single thing I had been relentlessly taught how to do. Now that this door was opening, I had to walk through it.

At Cadwalader I would be the only black woman, and one of only two black attorneys. Every time someone encountered me there, another prejudice that said blacks were unworthy would fall. Besides, I would wear a pinstriped suit, do challenging work, get paid a lot of money. What was the harm? I even imagined myself following in the footsteps of the businessmen in my past. Hadn't both of my grandfathers been businessmen? Wasn't commerce as essential to a people as art?

I concocted a dozen rationalizations for the decision I was making, and all of them had an element of truth, but the bottom line was that by now the only thing I felt I knew how to do was strive after success. Everything else had dropped away in a miasma of hectic choices colored by fear. Success, traditionally defined and measured, was all I had left. As long as I stuck to the path of tests and standardized scores and grades, nobody could take my competence away.

So I said yes to Cadwalader, coasted through my last year of law school, knowing that I would not have to prove myself again until I reported for work, and studied for the bar exam. I slept easily, more easily than I had in a long while, knowing that my future was finally laid out for me.

Rosewood-colored walls: this is what I remember most about my first weeks at Cadwalader, the soft and elegant sheen of the walls. Deep mahogany would have been too dark, pine was unthinkable, but this polished, pinky, understated rosewood tone was perfect for a firm that dated back nearly two hundred years, that included in its history as partners Henry Taft, brother to the President, and George Wickersham, a former attorney general, appointed by President Taft. It was about money for sure, but old money, making large quantities of it for people who had prepped at the right schools and gone on to the right colleges, people who were not just smart but connected. The firm was spread out across three floors, with winding wooden staircases gleaming with brass appointments. The effect was old-fashioned, clubby, insular. The hallways were curved, and you could not find someone's office unless you knew where you were going or unless you were led, and this gave the impression of intimacy and privilege, as if arrow-straight corridors would be too brazen, too businesslike, for these oh-so-exclusive men.

The atmosphere was undeniably and unabashedly male. Scenes of hunting hounds decorated the walls, along with ancient drawings of lawyers gone by and the inescapable portraits of former partners, of course all men. There had been one sole woman partner, who had supposedly been made partner in order to attract to the firm her very desirable husband. The lunch places favored by the partners rarely had any women in them, except for whatever few might have come in with me, and the office rituals and rhythms were all male ones. The attorneys loosened their ties in the evenings, later they took off their jackets, and later still they rolled up their sleeves, and you could see the partners and associates scurrying about like well-dressed clones of each other.

There were approximately fifty-five partners at Cadwalader in 1976, including the lawyers in the Washington office. Of this number, none were women and none were black. Among the associates — another sixty or so attorneys — two were black, one man and me, and there were six or seven women associates. Nationwide, around that time only 8 percent of all lawyers were women, with a far smaller percentage of minorities. Even now, as the number of blacks and women in the profession has steadily risen, there is still only one black partner at Cadwalader. The black man at Cadwalader when I was there was several years my senior, and though he nodded to me in the hall and even joined me for lunch several times, he was too busy to spend much time with me. I understood. Besides, it was not as if the two of us, even conjoined, would have made much of a statement. There were more women, however, and we did try to bond, getting together once in a while to discuss professional problems we had in common. But the habits of the partners were so ingrained that changing their attitudes toward women felt like rolling a large boulder uphill with a spoon.

For the first year, we associates rotated through three areas of our choosing, after which we were to decide what our specialty would be. I did rotations in Corporate, Trusts and Estates, and Tax. Trusts and Estates was the domain of a number of the preppy types. It was where many of the smooth and seemingly not overly bright lawyers ended up. Using their connections, formed either in childhood or at the right schools, these charmers handled discreetly the affairs of the rich. It was just one among many types of affirmative action for white men I would encounter in the corporate world, places where chummy guys who knew how to dress well, who knew the best places to have lunch, could be assured of a job that would give them a good life.

One partner fitted all of these characteristics, but he was actually quite bright as well. His son had graduated from Kent one year ahead of me, and as a token of goodwill toward that shared history, when I rotated through Trusts and Estates he invited me to lunch. He was a serious dandy. Fond of vintage bow ties and gold wire-rimmed glasses, he had impeccably coifed white hair and a vague English accent — a poster boy for an elderly Trusts and Estates lawyer. We were to lunch at his club. On the appointed day, while I waited in his office, which was the size of a studio apartment, he rang for his secretary to confirm the reservation. One other associate, male, was joining us.

"There will be three of us for lunch," he said to his secretary, "and one of us is a woman."

I thought this was self-evident, or at least I hoped that it was, yet this curious phrase was repeated as we made our way from the front door of the club to our table.

"Three for lunch," the partner said to the doorman, "and one of us is a woman." Similarly to the maitre d'. I later learned that women were allowed to eat only in certain dining halls, that they were not allowed to use the stairs that would take them past the private dining rooms but were steered to a special elevator set aside for members with female guests. There were entire floors where women were verboten. Still, this announcement puzzled and amused me. I kept imagining sentries running around the building like Paul Revere, shouting, "A woman is coming, a woman is coming!"

What, I wondered, would follow the cry? Were there men inside having their lunch with their trousers off? Were they swearing obscenities at the top of their lungs? And what further preparations were being made to the table where I would eat? Would a pink chair be brought in especially for me? Would the table itself be cordoned off?

But the table, when we arrived, was indistinguishable from the others, and though everyone looked up and stared at me as I passed, no one was doing anything untoward or obscene.

That stare, however, was one I had begun to associate with my foray into upper-crust establishments. It was a blatant stare, as if I were so much an object, or so much an intruder, that there was no need to hide the look, no need to be polite, because I was not worthy of or entitled to politeness. The stare transparently betrayed the thoughts behind it: Look at that, a black person. A woman. Look at that. And my God but she's tall. Perhaps she's a model. Who is that that she's with? Isn't that one of the Cadwalader partners? Good Lord, do you think she's one of their lawyers? Impossible. But then, what else could she be? A secretary perhaps. But no, look at that suit. And he would never bring a secretary here. So she must be a lawyer. Well, what do you know. Well, I pity them. She probably doesn't know how to write an intelligible sentence, much less a decent memorandum of law. What, good Lord, if she is only the first of many?

I could do nothing to interrupt this train of thought; it would proceed of its own accord. Yet I have to admit that my reaction to the stare was a feeling of triumph. It was a small triumph maybe, but I had invaded their private sanctuary and there was nothing they could do about it. I then noticed that the Cadwalader partner also seemed uncomfortable, so I tried putting him at ease. I talked of law, and Kent, and asked about his home and family. I could see him note that I knew how to use all of the utensils, and how to order as well. My triumph now felt secure. I was not what anyone expected. It should have been a paltry prize, but it gave me a certain revenge, and I began to look forward to these opportunities to confound expectations.

During encounters with other lawyers outside of the firm, I was never sure which disturbed them more, my sex or my race. The package came together, so it was hard to tell. Since beginning associates were rarely, if ever, taken to meet clients, most of my exposure was at professional functions: meetings of tax professionals, luncheons or workshops organized to discuss legal issues or trends. At all of these meetings, the attendees were overwhelmingly white and male. (Tax meetings had an extra dimension — most of the participants also were balding and smoked cigars. These two attributes seemed to be a job requirement for tax attorneys of which I was unaware.) Whether seated at a table or a lecture, or going into the dining room for lunch, I was usually mistaken for somebody else — a secretary, a waitress, anything but the professional I was — but that didn't really bother me. What did bother me was the looks of astonishment I received when I corrected the misperception that I was in the wrong place. More than astonishment: once again the looks conveyed outrage that I had invaded a private sanctum. The response gave me an odd sense of my body and my stature — as if I had so much more power than I felt myself to possess.

At one meeting, a luncheon on some economic topic, the keynote speaker was Malcolm Forbes, Jr. He was, of course, the son of Malcolm Forbes and the heir to his fortune. He was also the editor in chief of the magazine his father had founded, *Forbes,* which labeled itself (I always thought somewhat amusingly, given the rumors about Forbes Senior's sexual proclivities) "The Capitalist Tool." At any rate, Malcolm Forbes, Jr., took the podium and, before he began his speech, made a joke that alluded to the nepotism that had got him his job. It was something like, "Well, I guess knowing the right people put me where I am today," or words to that effect.

The hearty and self-congratulatory laughter that followed revealed the underside of the joke: Forbes's advantages were something that they knew they all shared. From the good health that had started in their well-nourished mothers' wombs to the connections they would rely on — such as calling up old Binky at Yale for a job for their son, or for themselves if they were out of a job — every step of their smooth path was dependent on familial advantage, none of it arising by dint of unaided effort alone.

And it was true for me too. Like them, I had been blessed with particular talents, but also like them, I'd had advantages that nourished those talents. Who I was now was inextricably linked to those advantages: the houseful of books, the Saturday trips to the library, the supportive community, the role models I saw everywhere I turned. I could tease not a whit of it out and say this or that accomplishment was all my own doing.

And yet, as I looked at these white men around me, laughing at Forbes Junior's self-deprecating joke, what I was astounded by was their public insistence, so at odds with this private face, on denying that any of this was so. Because it was part of the conservative white male mythology to maintain — to the death — that such privilege did not exist. Forbes could joke about the leg up he'd had and know that he would strike a familiar chord, because they'd all had that leg up too, and while they might boast about it here, largely among those they considered their peers, they would also, in another context, deny it.

The extent of this lie — of theirs as a world without special favors — struck me as monumental. I mean, here they all sat, suffused with a sense of entitlement, as if they had earned every bit of this space when they knew that this was simply not so.

This, then, was another thing that made the presence of someone like me so unsettling: it disrupted the game they were all so strenuously playing, the game in which they were on top simply because they were formed of the best stuff. It was not sufficient to have all of the material things that came with their favored position in life. They liked to pretend that the material wealth sprang, Calvinist style, from their intrinsic superior worth. If someone like me could also be one of the best, then maybe their stuff was not really the best. Furthermore, just the sight of me, whether I was actually worthy or not, forced them to confront what they had all agreed they would never publicly, admit: the fact of the immense privilege that being born white and male (and often well-to-do) conferred upon them. With me in the room they were forced to confront, and then disown, these numerous props that had brought them this far.

It was the second time in my life that I wondered if white people, or at least those in the grip of this illusion of their own mythic superiority, were truly insane, or if they hypnotized themselves every morning in order to believe the absurd things they did.

As all of this was going through my mind, someone interrupted my thoughts. People rarely spoke to me at functions like these. They stared at or talked about me, but did not address me directly. So I was startled when the man beside me spoke. "Are you a lawyer?" this man asked. That was all. He didn't say hello, or introduce himself, or even ask if I was enjoying the meeting. Just, was I a lawyer. There it was, that insanity again. This was, after all, a meeting of lawyers. I was sitting there in my pinstriped suit with my name tag and my briefcase, just like the rest of them.

No, I'm a terrorist, I wanted to say. I sneaked in here and am planning to blow you all up. But I didn't answer, just nodded, barely acknowledging him. I could see him out of the corner of my eye, leaning over to read my name tag. He was like a range rider, the border patrol, scouting the perimeter. But he could find nothing amiss, so he went back to his chair and let me remain. After the speech, which I didn't really listen to, I ate my rubber chicken and left.

Within the firm, it seemed that my sex was the more disturbing of my attributes, though in retrospect this may have been because there were only two black lawyers, so we did not raise the real specter of Black People, whereas there were enough female attorneys to raise the issue of Women, with a capital *W.* Or perhaps it was just easier for people to convince themselves that I was some sort of exception racially than it was to do that with gender. Whatever the reason, our female presence seemed to represent a deeper challenge.

The firm routinely held official functions at private clubs that did not admit women, and many of the partners were members of such clubs. There were no women partners, and though we associates were forming a bit of a nucleus at the bottom, there was no indication that any one of us would rise to the top. Some of the female associates, including me, got together and composed a letter to the partners, stating our belief that the firm's pattern of holding functions at places that discriminated against women undermined its nondiscrimination policy. It is hard to believe that Cadwalader is really committed to equality, we wrote, if it regularly takes us to clubs that, should we choose to go there on our own, would refuse us admittance. The partners were aghast. What did one thing have to do with the other? they shot back. They would hold the firm's functions wherever they chose.

For the women associates, the task was like that faced by the black professors at law school — to prove that you had what it took, in a system that was convinced it was impossible that you did. Here again, the qualities held in highest respect were intellect and aggression. And, oddly enough, submission as well. You were to abuse those who had less power, but you were also to toady to those who had more. It was a rigidly hierarchical system, and it confused most of the women. Many of us made the mistake of applying whatever approach we favored evenhandedly to those we worked with. So, if we were conciliatory, we were conciliatory with all, and if we were a bit reserved, as I was, similarly we were reserved to those both above and below.

In my Tax rotation I worked for two men. They were

opposites in personal style, but they were united in what appeared to me to be their deep disdain for the female sex. One I will call Tucker: he was tall and barrel-chested and never without a cigar. His office was like an English hunting lodge — the only things missing were the trophies from his latest kill. His furniture was all heavy leather. When we went out to lunch, Tucker usually ate great quantities of beef, and no amount of boarding school charm on my part could soften him up. I was a female, and therefore somewhat useless. Not useless in a narrow professional sense: he even began to respect my work, albeit begrudgingly. But it was not a respect that extended to my person. Whenever we were together, I could tell it was torture for him. If he couldn't fight me or bed me, I could tell, he didn't know what he should do in my presence.

The other partner styled himself after a European count of some sort. He had an affected way of speaking, as if he were so cosmopolitan and well traveled that various accents had adhered to his speech. He wore his hair clipped close to his head and sported a pencil-thin mustache that he constantly smoothed with his fingers. Unlike Tucker, who was terse and to the point in my presence, this partner, whom I'll call Cranston, dripped Old World charm. He welcomed me into a meeting as if I were a courtesan invited to entertain the guests. "Oh, Miss Parker," he would gush, "you are looking absolutely enchanting today. Absolutely enchanting." Then he would ogle me in what I presume he thought was an irresistible way. "That dress is most beguiling on you."

I remember one dress that elicited an especially enthusiastic reaction. It was pearl gray, soft wool, rather simple and longish, with big side pockets and a sash made of the same material. I bought it because I was tired of wearing the pinstriped suits day after day, and it was conservative and comfortable, and I thought wearing it would be a refreshing change. But after Cranston commented on it, I never wore it to work again. Not that he was deterred. A blouse was a fetching color. A scarf looked so lovely against my skin. Even a pin on my lapel was quite charming. With other men, of course, these partners were very different. With men, Tucker was like a roguish boy, rough-mouthed, full of jokes and laughter, and Cranston was straightforward, urbane and witty but reserved. It was not only the difference in their behavior that was so galling, but the singling out. It provided a clear signal to the other associates how we women were viewed.

Despite the presence of these two partners in the Tax Department, I ended up joining it at the end of my first year, primarily because it was the only department that had the right to pick and choose whom it would let in. Though the partners had not treated me with any great respect, they were pragmatists and invited me to join the department because they were pleased with my work. Even among the oversized egos of Cadwalader, the Tax Department was given a grudging place at the top: nerdy, bookish, physically unappealing as the people may have been, it was where the smartest attorneys were. To be in Tax, so went the firm's belief, you had to be not only smart but brilliant. If my being a black woman in a Wall Street firm was an anomaly, being in the Tax Department was even more so, and by now I was hooked on the adrenaline that flowed whenever I was where I was least expected to be.

One of the hardest things about working at Cadwalader was that I never found a partner with whom I could make a human connection. It was a new situation for me. I had always, in all other circumstances, found a way around the barriers of my purported difference, found some common ground to attach me to others. At Cadwalader, it was not that common ground did not exist, it was instead that the myths governing so many attitudes were like land mines rupturing that ground.

There were many such myths. The most obvious was that only white males could do the exacting intellectual work required by this high-priced law firm. More accurately defined, the original myth was that only white Anglo-Saxon Protestant males had the requisite and delicate combination of intellect and breeding to inhabit these corridors of power. Jews were new on the scene at many of these firms, their previous purported failing being one of breeding rather than intellect — a prejudice that sometimes surfaced in the offhand assessment of certain partners or associates that Jews were bright, admittedly, but a bit too aggressive and money hungry. The up-and-coming ethnics — the associates with Polish or Italian surnames — were also not sure of their place. One such associate I knew, who eventually became a partner, seemed to need to outdo the Wasps when it came to enforcing the rigid hierarchy that was so prevalent at the firm, and in sacrificing his personal life to prove his loyalty. As a black and a woman, I wasn't the only newcomer by far, but the myths about people like me were the antithesis of everything the firm's culture prized. I was presumed to be of inferior intellectual stock; my breeding was, by definition, not breeding at all; and I carried the taint of the field and the bedroom, both of those locales as far from the boardroom as could be. I raised these issues in this virulent way, out of keeping with the tenor of the times, because I was invading a terrain still largely perceived as exclusively white. Even when I was accepted on a personal level, under the surface my representational self was like ink sullying otherwise pristine waters.

Of course not everyone held these attitudes, and certainly among the associates I was able to make a few friends — although the workload was so heavy that friendships had little time to grow. And there was one male partner, a middle-aged man, who seemed to recognize my isolation and wished to alleviate it in some way. He made a few overtures, occasionally taking me to lunch and allowing the conversation to drift, however awkwardly and stiffly, onto personal topics. But standing between us was my sex and my color, conjoined in a particularly toxic brew. There was nothing even remotely sexual between us, just the fact that he was a man edging into middle age, and when he looked at me, he saw an attractive young woman. Had I been white, he would have done what other clear-eyed and upright men had done: made me over in his mind into the image of a daughter, a few years older than the actual daughters whose pictures I spied on his desk, so that the current between us would be transformed to a comfortable fatherly affection. But here was where my color stood in the way. It placed me irretrievably beyond the notion of daughter. And it evoked all those exotic myths that bespoke sex, preconceptions that, I could tell, as a man of principle, he was loath to admit were in the air. So we were never able to fumble our way past the most inane conversations to the common ground of simple humanity.

Like most big New York law firms, Cadwalader was a narrow-necked funnel when it came to advancement. Lots of eager young talent poured in at the top, precious few partners squeezed out the bottom. Some associates made the necessary sacrifices to put them in the running for the ultimate prize. Their personal lives went on hold. They worked weekends and late nights as a matter of course, never made plans that they couldn't, at a moment's notice, cancel. Their wives and girl-friends and boyfriends and friend-friends understood and accepted that their work, always and without fail, came first. But hard work alone was not sufficient. Any associate who hoped to succeed would have to find a partner willing to serve as a mentor, who would pass on not just the fine points of the law but the niceties of client appeasement and stroking, and above all the secret of rainmaking, that ability to bring new business into the firm. And if, with all of this, the associate was also well respected and liked by enough partners, he was now really in the running, and then it would be his patience and stamina that were tried, as he put in eight or nine or ten years before a partnership decision was made.

During my second year at the firm, I saw the first wave of casualties. One young associate confided to me that his new wife was already complaining: she never saw him, he left before she was barely awake and came home long after she was in bed, and for the few hours he was home on the weekend, he was distracted and tense. "I've tried to explain to her how it is," he said, "but she said the money just isn't worth it. She wants me to quit. I don't know what I should do."

His was not the only lament. The fiancée of another associate broke off their engagement after seeing the changes the firm had wrought in him and in their relationship. He, however, was cavalier. "I can always get another girlfriend," he said. "I can't just get a job like this every day."

For myself, I knew about the grind of billable hours, about what two thousand billable hours translated into, in terms of the number and length of days worked. Some of us even calculated what our great salaries worked out to on an hourly basis, and we discovered that we made less per hour than the more senior secretaries did. But if I was caught up in the race to succeed, I was also beginning to acknowledge its toll. I no longer knew how to relax, no longer knew how to take pleasure in things as I once had been able to do. Calls from friends became less frequent. I found it hard to tear myself away from the office, even when I could easily leave, because outside the office I would be forced to confront the shambles that my personal life was quickly becoming.

My parents would have been a natural place to turn for support, but at the time, they were embroiled in their own catastrophic change. After twenty-nine years of marriage, they had separated, as far as I could tell, irreconcilably. My mother was distraught and despairing, my father aloof and insistent that he was not to blame. Without their backing, I developed a brittle impatience that never let up. I was snappish with people who could not think as fast as I could, the way the partners thought nothing of cutting off someone who did not get to the point right away. I would likely have had a drinking problem if only I had been able to drink much hard liquor, but my constitution saved me from the vice that swallowed up many of my colleagues.

If I was unprepared for how quickly my personal life changed, I was also wholly unprepared for the gratuitous cruelty in the office, which seemed to be part and parcel of power. Secretaries were yelled at with impunity. Associates were routinely reminded of their lowly status. A partner could walk into an associate's office and interrupt for any reason, no matter how trivial. A partner would assign a memorandum to me on a Friday afternoon, telling me that he wanted it on his desk first thing Monday morning, and after a weekend of canceled plans I would deliver the memo on time, only to have it languish unread on his desk for days. Partners exploited their power because they could, and they seemed to enjoy it for the same reason.

I took it — we all did — and what surprised me was how quickly we could all be changed. Young men whose greatest offense was an overweening ego now strutted about the office, screaming at temps, interrupting each other, belittling the paralegals who worked for us. I might have taken it even longer if it had not been for one event, the annual Christmas party, usually held at the Plaza Hotel. (I had been absent from the firm for the one given my first year.) It was the only large function to which the so-called staff was invited. I assumed it would be like any other Cadwalader affair, a somewhat reserved event in a stultifyingly stuffy atmosphere that would end with too many of the partners and associates glassy-eyed from drink. However, by eleven on the morning of the event, I realized that something else was afoot.

The secretaries began disappearing from their desks, and the women's bathroom was awash in organdy and lace and toile and hair spray. It seemed as if they were spraying all day. Teasing and spraying and setting and spraying some more. They were transforming themselves, these girls from Queens and Brooklyn. For one night, they were going to be invited to the ball.

The party began, right after work, with dancing. Not sedate

waltzes or updated pop tunes played in three-quarter time, but rock-and-roll, belted out by a band that knew its job. In a great flurry, the secretaries and the partners and the associates got up to dance. Men who barely spoke to these girls in civil tones were now sweeping them onto the floor. No one asked the women attorneys to dance. We stood like wallflowers at a teenager's party — or, more aptly, like wives at a stag party. It was the alacrity with which it all began that told me that this was a practiced ritual that both sides had indulged in before. In a matter of moments, these former preppies were all drunken frat boys. They danced suggestively, they pulled the girls close. Watching them, I was reminded how some white boys at college danced to the blues, all thrusting of pelvis. A torrent of high-pitched giggles cascaded about the room.

I thought it was going to end with that — high-spirited flirting and a little charade of lust. But there was more. By the end of the evening one of the partners I worked for, so aloof and uncommunicative with me, had three or four girls on his lap. His hands went where they would. The next day, I overheard some of the partners boasting. "I had three in my room," they snickered, "how about you?"

Perhaps it was just idle boasting, but I doubted it. I had rationalized their despicable treatment of me and the other associates because, after all, we were buying into the game: we got the perks and the money, and if we hung in long enough, we might even get the power too. I didn't like the system, but still it had a small shred of ethics to it. Yet if conquests really had been made of these young women, it was like raping children. Those girls from Queens really wanted to be queen for a day. Seeing them preening and preparing, you knew there was a dream in it — a dream of a house in the suburbs, of lunching in places like those we lunched in every day, of fancy dinners. If they would not become wives, the ultimate goal, and certainly a fantasy even for them, they would at least be the mistresses, but they couldn't know that even that goal was out of their reach. The paralegals were the mistresses; the wives were the girls these men had met in college.

The morning after, I was summoned by a partner to receive an assignment. It was the same man who had had the secretaries on his lap the night before. He was standing outside his office when I arrived, and his secretary, as usual, called him by his surname. He called her by her first name, as if he took no notice of her, as was his habit. I wondered if those other secretaries would still call him by his surname this morning. But then, I thought, why wouldn't they? From his perspective, and in all the ways that really counted in the firm, nothing of substance had changed.

I could pretend, in hindsight, that I left Cadwalader for purely high-minded reasons, but the truth is that choosing to leave was the only decision I could make. I was like a swimmer whose lungs strained for breath after a deep dive. Perhaps I would have made myself over if I'd been able to, but I was missing too many of the requisite parts. A former colleague of mine told me many years later that a partner had once confided to her that the firm felt it had taken a great risk in hiring someone like me, because, as he put it, if I did not measure up, the firm would never be able to get rid of me. Even twenty years later, the comment called up in me a great surge of anger, and pride, the two mixing in toxic combination.

At the time that comment was made, when I was still at the firm, anger and pride were all I knew. The anger arose from my great rage at being rejected, a reaction to the unspoken but always present knowledge that people did indeed worry and fret over how I might be gotten rid of. And my fury was supported by a pride that was just as huge, that told me I was, in every way that mattered to them, their equal.

I was angry all of the time. Angry at the people I worked with, angry at the similarly suited and accessorized people I mingled with on the train I rode every day. I had moved to Connecticut in my second year at Cadwalader, to a small, trendy suburb on the shore, and my daily commute became a surrogate outlet for my dismay at my world. If these trench-coated men with their hard square briefcases thought they could deny me a place I had earned, I would show them. The trains were always crowded, and I invariably had to share my double seat. Without fail, the man sitting next to me would spread out his newspaper wide, encroaching on my space as if I weren't there. Or he would take up all the room on the seat, so that I had to tuck my arms in at my sides like a trussed chicken. Or if we were facing each other, he would spread his knees on either side of mine, forcing my legs into a tight space in the center. From behind me, people would unmindfully rest their newspapers on my head. I once deliberately took the same liberty, and when I did, not only the person I had offended but others nearby immediately assailed me with dirty looks. If I protested others' trespasses, as I occasionally did, I was clucked at as if I were crazy.

These minor offenses did in fact make me temporarily crazy. I became obsessed with this war over space. My friends began to give me strange stares when I recounted one battle after another. I would spend the commute with my elbows locked outward on either side of me, trying to defend my right to the borders of my own seat. I would kick out from under me the briefcases that were casually inserted beneath my feet. "Why don't you just get out of your seat and move?" some of my friends asked. But I couldn't let go. I was determined to remind these white men, in this private war, that the entire world was not theirs for the taking.

Of course, the battle was exhausting. I would no sooner be done with the man on the train than I would have to start with the man on the subway. And the partners in the office. And the other attorneys. And the staring men at the luncheons. *I am here, I am here, I am here. I am as smart, if not smarter, than you.* It was the tick-tock that came from my core. I was now the racial grenade, but what I was blowing up, over and over, was myself.

SIX

Uppity Buppie

I LEFT Cadwalader, Wickersham & Taft less than a year after the Christmas party. I had accepted a new position as a tax attorney at the American Express Company. My leave-taking was more a bolt than a considered career move, but even as I ran, I slowed down to consider the change. After all, two years at a place like Cadwalader could be put down to experience. This new job was a real commitment to a career in mainstream corporate America. I was twenty-eight at the time, old enough, I told myself, to have a more solid sense of direction. I had lunch with my old professor and friend from NYU, and when I told him of the new job I'd accepted, he asked me why I hadn't chosen to clerk for a judge instead. "Or think about politics or government service," he said. "You could make a real contribution."

Contribution. It was indeed a reverberant word. It was all that I had heard growing up, but it was a word I found increasingly confusing. I thought about my ancestors, living in a much more circumscribed world, and not by choice. How much easier it must have been for them to make a contribution, with every achievement redounding to their credit. How was a contribution going to be defined or measured in this much wider world?

"Well, business people make a contribution," I said, giving the answer I'd been practicing for a while. "Most of my family were businessmen."

"Really?" my professor asked.

I gave him the litany: my father, my grandfather, my great-grandfather.

"Back in Durham?" he asked, and I nodded. He took another bite of his lunch. "That's not exactly the same as American Express."

I shrugged in response. He was so sure of himself, and in this, he reminded me of my great-grandfather. I knew he was right, and at the same time his sureness frightened me. It seemed to call me to a task I wasn't ready to do. In the last few years I had gone through the motions, as if my real life were waiting for me in the wings. But now, for just a second, in my professor's eyes I saw that this life I was leading was real. And it was also a life, I could tell, that he found lacking. In my honest moments, I found it lacking as well. But the alternatives appeared just as daunting, as if the life that he led, like the one my great-grandfather had led, was too ardent and real. They stood on life's stage naked of props.

"Well, isn't this what we've been marching and protesting about?" I asked. "Making it possible for black people to go anywhere they choose?"

Now it was my professor's turn to shrug. "Is that what we've been struggling to do?" he quietly asked. I gave him my now commonplace rationalizations, and he accepted them.

And in place of any sureness about my decision, I focused instead on the sheer relief I felt to be leaving the firm.

I started at American Express in the fall of 1978. From a world that was stultifying and oppressively male, I was suddenly in a company that prided itself on its youthfulness and its energy, and whose ranks, at least at the middle-management level, were filling with women. Jim Robinson, the chairman and chief executive officer, was in his early forties, and the company's new hires, like me, bore faces that reflected the growing diversity of the American workforce. Where I'd had no delusions that a place like Cadwalader was about to change, hopeful signs of transformation were everywhere at American Express.

The first was in the look of the workplace at the start of the day. The firm had been all hushed, narrow hallways, but Amex Plaza was all marble and light. The headquarters overlooked the Hudson, at the very tip of Manhattan, a short lunchtime stroll to the Staten Island ferry and the Circle Line to the Statue of Liberty. I remember how it felt those first few weeks when I arrived at work each morning: the lobby abuzz with messengers and mailroom sorters and secretaries and junior managers and lawyers and senior executives, people from all over the city and from all over the world. Among the large workforce there were Hispanics and Asians and blacks, Pakistanis and Frenchmen, Barbadians, and Italians — everywhere faces that bespoke difference. It was easy, particularly in contrast with the strangled conformity of the firm, to imagine that this was truly a microcosm of America, that we were, in fact, creating the new American community.

Of course, at the upper reaches of the company, the faces were as nearly uniformly white and male as they had been at the firm. Still, the sheer number of us at the bottom and the middle who were different was cause for hope. Surely this diversity was not just happenstance; in our growing numbers there must have been a purposeful design. Perhaps all of our female and brown, black, tan, pink, umber faces were included not with reluctance but with real dedication to change.

Having my first female boss only accelerated and strengthened this fantasy. Finally I was working for someone I could not only learn from in a narrow, technical way, but for whom I had a large measure of personal respect. My new boss, Diane, was smart, professional, perfectionist in her approach to problems, and incredibly hard-working. She was also sweet, unfailingly polite, and easy to get along with. We worked well together, and when we had lunch together, as we often did, we could easily turn from business and relax.

My first few months at American Express were like a powerful antidote to my nearly two years at the firm. This, I hoped, was the real face of American business — no evildoers plotting the exploitation of the masses; instead, nice people, fun people even, pleasantly and for the most part respectfully doing their jobs. For the better part of a year, simple politeness was a welcome tonic.

Toward the end of my first year, Diane had scheduled a trip to Guatemala that she was unable to make because of a lingering ailment. Though I had not worked on the launch of the new credit card that was the occasion for the trip, Diane passed all of the files on to me and asked that I take her place on the trip. I eagerly took on the assignment. It was a challenge to get up to speed quickly on the issues, and I felt that this was the first time I would be doing a major task all on my own. The last-minute preparations and phone calls were exciting, and it was a heady feeling to jet off to a foreign country as one half of the legal team responsible for supervising the foreign counsel working on the launch.

When I arrived at the airport in Guatemala, I was met by the Mexican and Guatemalan attorneys and accountants who would be working with us. They had been told that another attorney was coming in Diane's place, and when they realized that I was she, there were the usual looks of surprise, not dissimilar to the looks I had grown accustomed to whenever I traveled on business for Cadwalader. The other attorney, handling the nontax issues, was also a woman, and our hosts did not disguise the fact that they found two women attorneys on one trip to be quite unexpected. "Both of you are women," they kept exclaiming.

"And both so tall!" another added. The fact that I was black was surely a second shock, but they did not comment on this. Instead, my height apparently became the surrogate. They all looked goggle-eyed at me. "You are really, really tall," they would each say when I caught them staring.

We proceeded from there to an all-day meeting. At first I was too engrossed in the task to notice the careful attentiveness when I had something to say, the solicitousness for my comfort, the smiles set on High, the casual deference. But midway through the meeting it dawned on me that there was a significant shift from the position I had occupied within Cadwalader. I was no longer solely defined by my race and my sex; I had now attained a stature inflated by the weight of the company I represented. My opinion mattered to these men: if they were charming and efficient and apparently competent, they wanted me to take note of those facts. For that would mean a positive assessment of them, and that in turn would mean that dollars from the company would continue to flow to them. It was a simple equation, but it represented my first experience of the power that accrues by virtue of position. At Cadwalader, no one had been beholden to me. I was at the bottom of the heap, and my opinions held no sway. Here I already possessed a certain status.

It was not an instantaneous transformation, but I was slowly seduced by the pleasant feeling of being treated as if I were somebody special. Not just smart or competent, but special at the core, as if formed from fine building material. I liked being in charge, liked having my awkwardness interpreted as judicious reserve. I discovered, in fact, that there were clear merits to me in this system that valued power above personality. As the tax attorney from American Express, I rose above being merely Gwen.

Concomitant with this shift in my status, there was a subtle shift in my attitude toward my job. I began to enjoy telling people what I did for a living. I liked the nods of approval that followed. I liked the expense-account dinners when I worked late, calling cabs to take me home, the company élan that rubbed off on me. I especially liked the new status I held within my family. Though my parents had been proud of my job at Cadwalader, it was a pride I could take no joy in because I found the workplace itself so depressing. Here I could bask in the pride without penalty. At family gatherings my father made sure everyone knew about my title and responsibilities, and with his encouragement I added tidbits about my business travels. Though I sometimes felt overwhelmed by the work-load, and Diane and I often groused to each other about it, the hours were nothing like the ones I had been expected to work at the firm. I even had time now to spend the good money I was earning. I began to believe that I had discovered a life I could settle into and enjoy.

During my second year with American Express I was placed in a program for preparing minority employees, both women and blacks, for senior-management positions. There were about ten of us in my group, all identified as "high-potential" minority employees. The course supposedly cost the company nearly ten thousand dollars per employee, and we were all encouraged to feel important by virtue of this investment.

We met once a month or so and were given assignments, such as to make a contact in a new area of the company we wanted to learn more about or to call up a senior manager and ask him or her to lunch. Afterward we wrote up our thoughts and impressions and shared them with the rest of the group, and the senior managers gave us feedback on our completed assignments. The program's purpose was to give us a better understanding of the culture we were part of, and point out when we did not understand its mores and rules.

I learned very quickly, for example, that my tendency to base relationships on whether I liked someone or not was wholly at odds with the culture. Relationships, I was led to understand, should be built around mutual goals and require-ments and power. By contrast, outside day-to-day projects, I rarely approached people for whom I had no natural feeling of sympathy. This reticence on my part, I learned, was interpreted as a lack of ambition.

An example of this lack of ambition was an incident cited by my boss's boss in which I had ridden the elevator with him one day and not taken the opportunity such access afforded. I had merely made small talk with him and then fallen silent. I had mistakenly seen the encounter as a purely personal one, and on a personal level, I had nothing much to say to him. I was later told that a white male who was ambitious would have seen this as a chance to ingratiate and impress, perhaps the time to regale the boss's boss with news of his work and his progress.

When an upcoming party was planned, we were asked to define our goals for the event. Not really believing that others went to a party with business objectives in mind, I asked three of my white male colleagues what their expectations were and was surprised when I received very specific answers from all three of them.

The course was an eye opener, but I found it vaguely depressing as well. Each month we sat and took copious notes on how to act like an ambitious white male. It apparently never occurred to anyone that we might have something to offer by acting out of our own traditions and backgrounds, and no one offered that as an alternative. Though I never expressed it, deep down I resisted the course. I did the assignments, expressed an understanding of the new concepts that were revealed, but despite my seeming acquiescence I assumed that I would be able to make my way in the company playing by my own set of rules. I learned to be more forthcoming with my superiors, relied less on my personal likes and dislikes, but continued to believe that if I merely did an excellent job, I would eventually be rewarded for that work.

Two years after I joined Amex, I transferred to the Office of Corporate Strategic Planning. I had learned in the management development program and through my experiences in the company that there was a major difference between staff and line employees. Those of us in the Legal Department were considered staff, well paid but essentially only helpers. Though my position brought me a certain status with outside vendors and outside lawyers, within the company the pecking order still placed me at the low end. Line positions were those with responsibility for making money for the company. I was advised by numerous people that if I was serious about moving up, I needed to shift to the business side.

I did indeed want to move up. During the spring of my first year at American Express, a small article on me appeared in *Mademoiselle* magazine. It was part of a regular feature that insiders at the magazine called "Real Girls," showing young career women on the way up, our photographs accompanied by brief comments about our goals along with details of where readers could buy the clothes and accessories we wore. In the picture I was suited for power, standing on a windy New York City street with my briefcase open and ready for action. My comments fit the image: I was a woman on the move, an ambitious corporate go-getter. If I had felt at the time that I was only pretending to be this person, by now my Real Girl ambitions had become quite real. I was growing fond of the treatment that said I was due a certain esteem and respect.

The Office of Corporate Strategic Planning was a perfect

segue from the law to the more prestigious business side. The office was the brainchild of Harry Freeman, a brilliant and somewhat eccentric man whose mind was forever in motion. Harry had spawned the idea of "cause marketing," the marriage of art, commerce, and philanthropy, a clever marketing device that linked using the American Express card with donations to charity and with an overall feeling of doing good. It took someone like Harry to carry off the idea of forming a cadre of thinkers for senior managers — their own little think tank that would explore the viability of new business ideas.

We were an eclectic crew, drawn from a variety of backgrounds and disciplines, all dedicated to that precious eighties notion of synergy — that out of the combination of disparate things would emerge something greater than the whole. There were several Ivy League M.B.A.ers, a line manager from Marketing, a former engineer, and me, a lawyer with a tax specialty, like Harry himself. My strengths — I had an analytical mind and approach to problem-solving, and had had training that could be turned to any number of challenges — were tailor-made for someone like Harry, a generalist who felt he could solve any problem that he unleashed his intellect and imagination upon. So I was selected. The employee newsletter trumpeted that this was the first director-level job ever to be filled through job posting. My career as an erstwhile businesswoman was born.

With this job came an intense camaraderie, a new experience for me. Harry believed in brainstorming, and almost daily he held staff meetings where we all sat around the conference table, throwing out ideas and endlessly debating their merits and demerits. We each had our special area of expertise. Because Harry was brilliant, we were supposedly all brilliant too, and there were indeed some certifiable geniuses among us. Kimberly, a young woman from Yale, was the uncontested brain of the group. She was quiet, unassuming, and there was nothing she did not know. Any question that Harry might ask — and he had a penchant for asking questions constantly on anything and everything — Kimberly knew the answer to it: the trading price of the stock of some start-up company, the uses of fiber optics, the latest price-earnings differential of a competitor. She never seemed to go home — at 7 A.M. she was there and at 11 P.M. she was there. If she hadn't been so nice, her brilliance might have caused a great deal of envy, but she simply knew everything there was to know, and that was that. Because she so firmly occupied that spot, we all sought other ways to distinguish ourselves.

A young line manager who briefly shared an office with me was the one with the practical information of our ongoing smaller-scale marketing efforts. One of the Ivy League M.B.A.s was always impressing everyone with her command of strategic buzzwords and charts of analysis. My forte was synthesis and creativity. I knew almost nothing about business per se, and even less about balance sheets and the like, but I had a knack for recombining things into a hitherto unconsidered new whole. It meant I was quiet for long stretches of time, but every once in a while I had something to say to which others wanted to listen.

Equally exciting to me was how the sphere I was operating in had expanded. As a lawyer, I had been a kind of technician, responsible for a range of issues but ones that covered only a narrow field. Here in Strategic Planning, however, we were led to believe that we were helping to chart the future of the company, and in that future lay the destinies of thousands of people. My great-grandfather, Dr. Moore, had been concerned with several things in his work at the Mutual. But most important, he made sure that the institution provided a needed service for blacks who may otherwise have been deprived of such service, since it was a practice at the time for mainstream insurance companies to temporarily suspend the coverage of Negroes or not to provide coverage at all. He also wanted to provide jobs and the means of a dignified livelihood for many Negroes who had few opportunities to rise to management positions. And he wanted to illustrate to Negroes themselves what they were truly capable of achieving. Similarly, in Strategic Planning I felt I was being shown the grand design of the company: what the world of integrated financial services might mean to the average consumer, the thousands of back-office jobs that future expansion would create, the promise of quality service that the company strove to uphold.

It was in Strategic Planning that I began to fall completely for the lure of the company. It was not at all dissimilar to falling in love. Suddenly words like "synergy" and "future trends" and "the global village" took on a new hue: they were the harbingers of a new world order, based not on the hegemony of old, outmoded distinctions among people, but on a true meritocracy that would span the world. I now wanted to advance not only for personal reasons, but because I believed I was helping to usher in a wave of change that was sweeping the company and all of American business. Much of the optimism about this purported future was due to Harry Freeman's influence. In addition to his job as cochair of the Office of Corporate Strategic Planning, Harry was also the head of Corporate Affairs and Community Relations, and in this role he was a master at finding the intersections of the company's interests and those of the larger community. Amex sponsored art exhibits and musical performances, funded soup kitchens and programs to develop minority interns. It was easy, under Harry's sway, to imagine that these dual interests of profit and community service were of equal importance. This farsightedness also extended to his personal style. As a manager, Harry was indifferent to color and gender — in fact, he was indifferent to most things that other people paid attention to. I never once, in his presence, felt like "the black woman" or "the black director," though I was the only black director in the group. All that appeared to matter to Harry were ideas, and if you had a good one, he wouldn't have noticed if you'd presented it in the nude.

His style was infectious, and these were exhilarating times for all of us. We had access to senior management in the form of early morning meetings. We went on countless retreats, where we brainstormed from six o'clock breakfast until long after dinner, sometimes as late as midnight. Our heads began to nod while Harry, as indefatigable physically as he was intellectually, still held court, throwing out ideas, assigning topics that someone would read up on for the next day.

As my allegiance to the company deepened, I couldn't help but hearken again and again to my great-grandfather. When I joined American Express, I halfheartedly wondered if I would uncover the zeal he had brought to the many business ventures he encouraged. Now I thought I had discovered the secret that lay behind his passion. My great-grandfather had been sure that he could combine an entrepreneurial mission with a collective social mission, and in the zest that Harry brought to his work, I perceived the same kind of passion. That's the kind of business person I want to be, I decided, and with this decision my larger ambition was born. Already the novelty of being treated with deference was starting to pale, and I needed a new reason to work. Finally I'd found it. My job was no longer just a place to pump up my somewhat bruised ego from the Cadwalader days, a place to hang out and do interesting work for which I was well paid. I now wanted seriously to get ahead, as far as I could go, in the company.

On one of our many retreats, I remember sitting at breakfast one morning bleary-eyed, not so much from lack of sleep as from constant togetherness. Harry was reading the *Wall Street Journal,* as was everyone else at the table, and he talked aloud as he read, commenting cryptically on those things he found of interest, giving us random assignments to follow up on something or other. As usual, his interest ranged widely. To me he mentioned a regulatory change that he thought might have significance for the company.

Harry's remarks were not new to me. In my days as a lawyer, I had often followed legislative trends to see what effect laws would have on the company's interests, so that we could try to influence the outcome in our favor. But now I saw for the first time the single-mindedness with which he approached his work. We were discussing an issue of general public interest, and though we were exchanging different arguments that could be made to support a particular position, it was apparent that the underlying public interest, in Harry's mind, was a poor relation: he gave it only secondary importance, if that. Instead, all of Harry's far-ranging interests, from art to politics to social policy to legislation, were subsumed to the one goal that counted within the company — namely, how to increase the bottom line. And why shouldn't that be so? Wasn't that what American business was about? Nevertheless, the absurd simplicity of his preoccupation shocked me. Unknowingly, I had so thoroughly absorbed the ethics of the business world I knew as a youth that I had grafted those beliefs onto this new environment, even as the evidence of major differences between the two rose before me.

Sitting there with my peers, I felt as if the skin of a common perspective that had bound us as a group had been unceremoniously ripped from me. Did anyone else feel as I did? At Cadwalader I had been set apart by the obvious differences of my race and my gender, but here I saw that something else set me apart: the values I'd been bequeathed in my youth.

Through the window I could see that it was a beautiful day, green and springlike. The landscape was lovely, with rolling hills and mature trees off in the distance. As I looked at Harry, so wholly immersed in this game of business, I saw that he was as oblivious of the physical surroundings as he was of any personal details about us. That he was truly, thoroughly engrossed in this discussion and its central aim. And more important, that this was a genuine passion for him. That where he was was exactly where he wished to be.

And I knew that none of this was true for me. Not once in the two-plus years I had been with American Express had I awakened with the company's fundamental purpose in mind — to make more money. In fact, the quarterly earnings was a figure I had trouble remembering at all. I would memorize it for an upcoming meeting, then forget it as soon as the meeting was over. I wasn't in the least interested in growth curves and quarterly earnings and price-earning differentials and all the other buzzwords I labored to keep straight in my head. Instead, I enjoyed the people I worked with, I worked on interesting problems that captured my attention, and I particularly enjoyed the places where the company's mission intersected with that of the larger community. But about the money Amex earned per se, I realized I really didn't care.

In a social history called *Black Business in the New South,* my great-grandfather was quoted as saying that there was a "larger truth" than just getting more business, and that at any point, should that truth and his business collide, then it was the business that he was prepared to let go. At my job there was no such conjoining of aims. If I was going to move forward in the company, I would have to organize my work life, and my motives for participating in it, around the sole, stark motive of profit.

While I was in the Office of Corporate Strategic Planning, I was named a Black Achiever in Industry. The award, part of a program sponsored by the Harlem YMCA, in association with a number of corporations, gave black boys and girls models of achievement in the corporate world by honoring black men and women who had succeeded. Participating companies purchased tickets for young people to attend the formal dinner and awards ceremony, and the entire evening was designed to showcase existing black talent and nurture future achievers.

My guests at the dinner, all seated at my table, were the

most important people in my life. My parents and my older brother and his wife were there, as was my grandmother Parker. (My grandmother McDougald had died of cancer during my third year of law school.) Several of my old Kent friends were there, as well as several new friends. My immediate boss from Strategic Planning was also in attendance. I sat next to my mother, and my father sat across the table from us, next to his mother. My parents, who had separated while I was at Cadwalader, now were recently divorced.

Despite the happy event, I remember being overtaken by an almost unbearable sorrow — sad that my parents had divorced, sad over my grandmother McDougald's absence. Even my grandmother Parker, though she was still going strong, no longer seemed as indomitable as she had to me as a child. And beyond these losses that I could do nothing about were those I saw looming in a future I was helping to create. I looked at all of the young brown faces arrayed around the bright room. They shone with excitement, maybe with dreams for their future, dreams that were being nourished by someone like me. I suddenly had an urge to run to each of them and warn them of the disappointments this life held. I was being honored as an achiever, but I couldn't help thinking, What had I achieved? Whose life had I changed for the better? Whose path had been cleared by my efforts? I was ostensibly making a way for these young people to follow behind, but follow behind to do what? I felt like the Pied Piper, blowing lovely music to lead these bright-eyed children off the side of a cliff. If they joined me at American Express one day, what legacy, beyond an increase in profits for the people who had invested in the company, would we all leave behind? I looked at my mother, who had taught thousands of young people. I looked at my grandmother, who had touched countless lives with her generosity. My father, as a pharmacist, had brought relief from suffering, and his wise counsel as a social worker had helped many people in need. Yet despite these differences, all of them were proud of this path I was on. In their minds, I too had achieved something. I had proved what it was that we as a people were capable of. It was a goal that I intimately understood, but as I sat there, I wondered if it could really be enough for a lifetime.

Despite my misgivings, my career seemed to continue of its own accord and with its own momentum. After less than eighteen months in Corporate Strategic Planning, I received my second promotion, to yet another prestigious department, in a new subsidiary formed after American Express acquired the Shearson brokerage house. And another year and a half later, my third promotion came through. This last job carried with it a staff and a budget, and I was out of specialized departments and into the world of line management.

My new department was in an area called service-establishment marketing. A service establishment was a retail business that accepted the American Express card. And just as the card-marketing people strove to expand the number of American Express cardholders, service-establishment marketing was concerned with expanding the number of places that accepted the card, as well as increasing the number of times that the card was used at each establishment. It was not the glamorous side of the business, but it was the profit engine of the credit-card business, and as a result, we were all paid very well.

With this new job, I was introduced to the mainstream of

middle management. As was the case in each of the departments I had been in previously, I was the only black at the director level. But whereas the other groups had been special, in that they attracted the exceptional talent in the company, this group contained many seasoned middle managers that were more typical of the company as a whole. It was where I soon learned of the key double standard that separated blacks from whites.

In this marketing unit I discovered what I referred to as the average white guy: the guy who worked reasonably hard but without killing himself, who was smart without being brilliant, who was personable without being Mr. Charming. Because the new job sprung me from my cocoon of special units, I began to interact with dozens of my peers throughout the company, where I learned that this typical white male was in plentiful supply. In fact, there were literally hundreds of them, all doing their jobs in an adequate way. They had gone to good enough schools, gotten adequate grades, and now had good jobs that allowed them to move up a few notches in salary every year.

What I found astonishing was that no one expected them to be anything other than ordinary. No one expected them to be outstanding or superlative — just competent was enough. And this averageness galled, because it had never been an option for me. As a black, being average was not nearly enough — I had to be better, and my credentials had to precede me, as if necessary to justify my mere presence.

I began to scrutinize more carefully the backgrounds of my counterparts within the company. I thought back to the two other black women lawyers I'd worked with in the Legal Department and realized how similar our upbringings had

been: all of us from well-to-do families, all of us schooled at Ivy
League colleges and good law schools, and all three of us
products of private prep schools. There were certainly other
lawyers in the company with similar credentials. But where, I
began to wonder, were the blacks with the more average
backgrounds, those counterparts of the many whites who fit
the average description. The common perception among people outside of such corporations as American Express was that
affirmative action meant a lowering of standards, but as I
looked around the company, almost invariably what I found
was just the reverse: the blacks tended to be better trained,
more competent, and brighter than their average white counterparts. It was the old Southern adage at work: you don't have
to be as bright as a white person to get the same job, you have
to be brighter and work twice as hard.

Now I noticed other things as well. If we black employees
had similar backgrounds, then that made us fit neatly into the
dominant culture. We even looked the part. I was brown-
skinned, for example, but with sharp features. My lawyer
colleagues were both very light-skinned. Many of the blacks I
met also had a low-key, nonthreatening, nonethnic manner.
Where was the great leap of faith in hiring and promoting
someone like me? How did my success alter the fortunes of
those who were much less lucky than I?

It was while I was in the thick of these thoughts that I began
to hear of another black lawyer who had recently joined the
company, Ken Chenault, who at that time was in the card
division. When we finally met, I could see why his name always
came up when somebody met me, as if something in the sight
of me spontaneously brought Ken to mind. Some of it was

superficial: he was a handsome brown-skinned man, I was an attractive brown-skinned woman. We both had Harvard on our résumés, mine for undergraduate school, his for a law degree. We both were lawyers who had moved to the business side. But what I was struck by when I first met Ken was a similarity below the surface. Both of us were entirely at ease with white people. As blacks in a largely white environment, we knew that part of our job was to put the white people we worked with at ease, to allay their tensions around us, and I saw in Ken someone whose skills, in this department, rivaled my own. And Ken had an additional skill, which people often called his smoothness. As I saw it, that smoothness came from his recognition that his ease with white people was not merely a neutral ability, but something he could turn to his advantage.

It was shortly after I met Ken that his first big promotion came through. He was named an executive vice president, a leap out of middle management to senior management. It was the dividing line we were all pressing toward, that mythical place where you did not just throw weight around, but you began to throw serious weight. It was also the color and gender dividing line. Up to the level of manager, the level just below my own, there was plenty of diversity in the ranks. At the director level, the group thinned considerably, particularly in terms of minorities, though there were still quite a few women represented. And at the vice-presidential level and above, there was yet another thinning. I watched Ken from afar, as if he were my doppelgänger. He had an advantage by virtue of gender, but more than that, he had a motivational edge. Unlike me, he did not appear divided in his goals, nor was he ambivalent about what it would take to achieve them. He was not

Machiavellian or sinister, he simply understood the rules of the game and was willing to play them. By contrast, I was still straddling the fence, not at all certain that I wanted even to be part of the game.

If the universe had conspired to teach me a critical lesson about my world and the toll it would exact from me, it could not have chosen a more perfect person to deliver it than Frank Partels. Frank at that time was a senior executive of the card and service-establishment marketing divisions. He had come in as a senior executive from Citibank. It was rumored that before he left there, disgruntled employees had riddled his car with bullets. I cannot claim to know the reasons for his rise or the true reasons for his demise. I only know the man that I saw during that time.

My first exposure to Frank was at one of the dreaded fortnightly business reviews that were his principal tool of management. Directors and vice presidents were required to make presentations at these meetings, at which Frank would ask questions — or rather, Frank would use the meetings to perform a ritual bloodletting. I heard about these reviews from my colleagues after they came staggering back to their desks. Under Frank's pitiless gaze, no one escaped unscathed. Everyone was incompetent and stupid. No one in his domain had the slightest idea of what they were doing. One colleague of mine, an equable man who was hard to ruffle, left one of these meetings looking as pale as a ghost. Another colleague, who was a twenty-year veteran of the company, merely said: "I have never seen anything like this. I am going to call Personnel tomorrow and start looking for something else." My own boss, it was said, had been humiliated when Frank purportedly asked her, "Where did you get your M.B.A.?" When she answered him, he said, "Remind me never to hire anyone from there again."

In between meetings, all the directors and vice presidents did was prepare for the next one. They wrote and rewrote, and their bosses corrected and slashed, until the dreaded day arrived and another group of us were herded toward our encounter. At the meeting for my section, when it was my turn to speak, I stood up and could feel the rivulets of sweat running down my arms to my elbows. It was late in the day, nearly six-thirty, and mindful of the long hours everyone had already put in, I started off with these words: "It's been a long day. I can see that everyone is starting to get tired. I will try and keep this as short and concise as I can."

Here Frank interrupted me. "Don't make any assumptions," he snapped. "I will tell you how fast or how slowly I want you to go."

I felt as I had when a madman once accosted me on the subway on my way to work. He had been a huge, muscular man, clearly disturbed, and in his derangement he fixed his rage at the world on me. I had believed he might kill me, and something had compelled me to meet every aggressive move of his with one of my own. I had sensed that my fear was the thing he needed, the blood that he sought to make his own warm. I felt the same thing now with Frank; he fed, like a shark, on others' fear.

"Well," I said to Frank with a laugh, "I was simply trying to be cognizant of the time. But if you want to tell me how fast or how slowly I should go, well then, you can just go on and do that."

The words were coming out of my mouth, but I was

actually as surprised by my cavalier stance as I had been by my similarly feigned toughness with the psychopath on the subway. It was not at all how I felt. But Frank sat up and took notice, as if I were a worthy opponent. He grilled me, and I continued my ruse. When I didn't know something, I casually admitted it and said I would get back to him. When he challenged me, I noted his objections with a slight shrug. Though I felt sickened by his free-ranging cruelty, the same instincts that had propelled me to this juncture in my life were taking over again. I returned his aggression with a subtle rage of my own, and gave him a bit of his own arrogance and cockiness back. I left the meeting still affecting a jocular mood, and my colleagues patted me on the back for my performance. Inwardly, what I felt was disgust. That I could play the game so well suddenly didn't feel like a skill of which I was particularly proud.

At another meeting with Frank, I watched him speak and began to fantasize putting a bullet in his brain. He had a large, high forehead, and it seemed to glisten as he talked, and I played the fantasy over and over in my head. This precise hole, this speck of blood, this look on his face before he would fall. After his speech, I ran to a colleague of mine and confessed my thoughts, afraid that I was losing my mind, and she grabbed my hands in hers.

"I was imagining stabbing him," she admitted, as if she too could not believe that such thoughts could lodge in her mind.

The bloodletting and the stirring up of my own aggression went on for well over a year and a half. Seasoned, competent people were fired, others begged for transfers. Work in the department nearly ground to a halt. A new senior vice president was brought in, ostensibly to lighten up Frank's style, but no one could change the course he had set. Eventually, but long after it felt timely, he was gone.

Shortly after Frank left, I was up for a new job, that of special assistant to the president. I hadn't applied for it. I was one of two candidates who had surfaced through a mysterious internal search. It was really a vice-presidential slot, the kind of steppingstone that could lead to heading up a whole department. For two years or so I would give my life to Lou Gerstner, president of the Travel Related Services Corporation, the subsidiary that housed all of American Express's traditional businesses — the card, travel, and traveler's cheques divisions — and in return I would receive the kind of training and access that no other job could supposedly match. I would be his right hand, searching out information for him, following up with division and department heads on things he wanted done. I imagined I would be like the young assistants to the president who ran around with walkie-talkies attached to their heads — filled no doubt with my own importance, receiving the kind of deference and respect that had nothing to do with me. People would return my phone calls first, and line up to talk to me at parties. Whenever I spoke, people would stop to listen.

It was not a job I would ever have applied for. It wasn't even one I was sure that I wanted. I had met Lou Gerstner a few times, and frankly I was uncomfortable around him. There was a calculating reserve to him, smoothed over by an affability that unnerved me. I could more easily imagine myself working for Jim Robinson, the chairman, whom I had also met a few times, who had a courtly Southern manner that was more familiar to me. Gerstner, I thought, could shoot you as easily as smile at you, and though I have no idea whether this distant impression I had of him was true, it was how I felt about him.

I was also worried about the commitment the job would require. At least monthly I complained to my friends how unfulfilling I found my work, but still I hadn't worked up the courage to go. This job, I imagined, would force me to marry the world I had been flirting with for so long. I would either have to make that kind of commitment or fail.

My interview came after the one for the only other candidate for the position, a white woman named Abby, who was also a director in my department. Abby was a steady performer with a quiet, assured manner and a seemingly unambivalent view of her work. I wondered if she had felt as nervous when she walked into Gerstner's office as I now did. The wraparound view of the harbor and the skyline behind his desk was dizzying. I wondered what it would be like to come into such an office each day. We sat on the sofa — or rather, I did, and he sat in a side chair. The sofa was low, and since my legs are long, I had the choice of stretching them out underneath the coffee table like a colt or keeping them primly together, risking raising my skirt too high. I opted for coltish, my legs extended somewhere off to the side.

Throughout the interview, I could tell that neither of us was comfortable. Gerstner tried to put me at ease, but he was not good at chatter, and we had no common plane on which to reach each other. I thought of all the jobs I had gotten before, and the roles I had played, the just familiar enough opening that each of my former bosses had given me. And with him I could find none. I tried being earnest and bright, but there was a steeliness in him that I kept thinking I was missing.

Moreover, I felt certain he could detect my lack of resolve.

Despite all this, I still expected to be offered the position. I expected it because I had been getting the jobs that I had applied for all my life. The schools, the grades, the jobs, they had fallen in line as they should, and I didn't think this would be different. Besides, there were only two of us in the running, both from the same department, and my background was more varied.

The phone call came just as I was getting ready to go to a colleague's farewell party downstairs. It was someone from Personnel. "I thought you would want to know," she said, "before you go to the party, before someone else says something to you. Lou has decided to go with Abby for his assistant. He thought you were great, and it was a difficult choice, but he thinks Abby, right now, is the one for the job."

"OK," I said. "Thank you for calling. I am just honored to have been in the running." I hung up and momentarily thought that I had dreamed the call. But no, I was sitting in my office, I was awake, the phone was back in its cradle.

"Are you coming to the party?" someone asked me, passing by my office. I wondered briefly if it would be possible to get out of the building without seeing anyone. I felt just as I had that day long ago when my teacher accused me of plagiarizing my poem, as if I had been reduced to something worthless, hardly able to breathe. It was as if the one thing I had steeled myself against had finally happened: I had gone head to head with a white person and lost. I tried to tell myself that it was not a big deal, that there would be other jobs, that the job wasn't something I had ever really wanted. But none of my consoling phrases penetrated to where failure was now sounding out like a clock gone awry. Failure, failure, failure, it tocked. There was suddenly no distance between the best and the worst, no in between, just succeeding or failing, with the latter feeling something like death. I realized that if someone had asked me a moment before the phone call had come, "How will you feel if you don't get the job?" that I would have been badly mistaken.

All along I had thought my desire to do well, to succeed, was a desire to prove what we as blacks were capable of. Now I was face to face with another, more secretive purpose, the need to lift myself above all the hurts that had been inflicted because I was black. Below was where they were all stored: the wounds inflicted by teachers who did not acknowledge my hand in the air, who took no delight in me; the scars left from partners of the firm who had never wanted to hire me; the chasm left by friends I had lost for the color of my skin; the pain of other brown people spurning me for being too brown, or too dicty or proper. They were all there, all below, and I had kept them all out of reach with this relentless quest for perfection. So long as I never failed, they could not touch me.

And now, finally, I had. I was no longer above them but on level ground, stripped of any pretense that I floated above. I went to the farewell party, my ears ringing, all of the voices too loud in my head, every laugh a laugh that sounded as if it were chosen just for me. I managed to congratulate Abby, said bon voyage to the guest of honor, and left as soon as I was able, as soon as it wouldn't have looked conspicuous. On the train ride home, I cosseted myself with chocolate and beer, until I was safely at home. When I got there, I cried and I cried and I cried.

*   *   *

Later, much later, I would be grateful to Lou Gerstner for not picking me. I would be grateful for his part in hastening the end of a ten-year detour in my life. But more immediately, what I was grateful for was the opportunity of learning what really motivated me, with what string I was really strung. In the days after not getting the job, the department I was once a part of was slowly dismantled. There would be a major reorganization, and I was assured of my place in the new division by the senior manager coming in. I learned that an old colleague of mine from one job ago would be my boss. I watched all of the events at a strange remove, as if they were happening to somebody else.

I knew that Lew, my soon-to-be boss, had not risen above me on sheer talent alone. He was one of those who'd gone to Christmas parties with his business objectives firmly in mind. He did not fall silent in front of a boss as I sometimes did. He was cheerful and bright and presentable and knew how to sell himself well. And just as he possessed advantages over me, there were others, still outside the company or passed over within it, over whom I had advantages: the smart, hard-working black woman who did not have an Ivy League school on her résumé to make the person hiring her feel confident about the "chance" the company was taking; the white ethnic who looked and acted ethnic; the black man with a chip on his shoulder. I saw it all — the myriad divisions and the ways people passed one another by. The days turned in a slow whirl, and I looked anew at this self I had willingly created, as if I had never seen her before.

Who was the I that could cry over not getting a job that I hadn't even wanted? Who was this person in the pinstriped suit? I always thought she had been created merely to take the easy way out, to avoid the hard choices that came with adulthood and growing up. Now I was learning that she served another purpose: in this artificial self, all of the pains and sorrows of my real self were kept at bay.

Everywhere I looked, it was as if things I had not seen were coming to light. I realized that not only did I not care about making money, but the one thing I did care about at American Express, the simple meaningfulness of people sharing a task, was the thing that was viewed as expendable. Frank Partels may have been an anomaly — few people in the company were as ruthless and cavalier in their disregard for other humans as he — but his rise was not an innocent one. His disregard for others was known, and the position he achieved was testament to the fact that as long as someone was viewed as productive, he was allowed to be abusive as well. There was no larger principle of restraint as my great-grandfather had felt, no overarching vision fostered by a solid and deep sense of community, no ethos that dictated to a man of luck and privilege that it was his blessing to be able to serve. There was only the dictate of the bottom line, and it was the only god we could fail.

For me, the only thing left in the company that had value was the people who worked there. Not for who they were, or for the power they held, but for the very personal fact of their humanity. For the first time in my life, during my years with the company, I had enjoyed being part of a group. The ties were not the intimate ones of family or friendship, but they were familiar ones nonetheless, like backyard neighbors in a gossipy town, our habits apparent to all, our foibles known and accepted. In the daily spectacle of our vivid array of humanity, all shouldering a common wheel, I'd found something tender and moving. And it was that vision that had tied me to the company, after all of my other reasons had failed. With its final fading, I knew it was time, as my great-grandfather had long ago said, to let the company go.

EPILOGUE

A Black Homecoming

AT THE AGE OF thirty-six, with a decade of professional experience behind me, a decade or more of schooling and training, I finally let go. I quit my job and dropped out of the life that I had carefully built, the life that had given so much satisfaction to my family, the life that for so long had seemed inescapable. In the process I dropped into what I had always wanted most to do with my life. I had never been able to keep the company's earnings in mind, but I had never forgotten, not once, the feel of a pen across paper — how it had felt to make lines that held meaning, how it had felt to be part of a dialogue with distant people across both space and time.

All along, I'd had two visions before me: one that contained this path I was on, and one of a life that would combine all of me, not just my intellect but my passions and values. Pursuing success, I had composed a life that was shaky at best, its foundations unstable, its design both shallow and narrow. It was an existence whose rewards were insufficient for a lifetime.

So I thought up my plan, called Personnel, made my appointment, and waited. It took another few weeks or so. Meetings back and forth. Documents I would have to review and then sign. But as of March 1986 I got what I sought: out. It was out with a severance package and the use of an executive outplacement firm for a year, or until I found a new job, whichever came first. After the papers were all signed, I confessed to the outplacement firm's manager that I did not actually desire another position, that what I wanted and intended to do was write. I had my current salary and benefits, under what was called an extended-notice provision, for another seven months, an amount of time that would prove to be ridiculously short.

It would be nearly six years before I completed my first novel and sold it to a publisher. In the intervening time I would work as a lobbyist, a marketing consultant, even as a lawyer again, though it was never for the same kind of clients or with the same kind of need. I lobbied for welfare mothers, helped small businesses incorporate, designed marketing plans for domestic-violence shelters, and advised older divorced women on their wills and their taxes. In my spare time I learned to make soups and African stews. I cultivated a cottage garden, and after many long years learned the meaning of patience. I no longer had a career that anyone envied. At parties, upon hearing what I did for a living, no one settled in for a chat. I still enjoyed eating in fancy restaurants, but I no longer had any need to do it to prove that I could.

It would be ten years before I looked back to tell this story, and there were two codas to this tale, each fitting the disparate halves of my life. The first occurred as I was finishing the first draft of this book. I went back to visit American Express, to see my old colleague Ken Chenault. Ken was now the president of Travel Related Services Corporation and vice chairman of all

of American Express. His career was proceeding just as everyone had predicted it would. And he was still young — life was
still an open plain spread out before him. I wanted to see him
for two reasons: to touch base and let him know, as a courtesy,
that this memoir would be forthcoming, and for a secret reason
that I could scarcely confess to myself — to see if the choice I
had made was the right one.

I went to see him on an early fall day, just starting to turn
cool, a little blustery as it always was at the tip of Manhattan. I
was wearing a borrowed coat that flapped about my legs in the
wind. For the previous year I'd been in South Africa, where it
was now summer, and I was back in the States for only a brief
trip. I was nearly late for our meeting because I'd forgotten
how big the World Financial Center's lobby was, how far I had
to walk from the curb to the elevators, and then, once I'd gone
through all of the security screening, how long it took to ride
the elevator to the fiftieth floor.

As I'd expected, Ken was on the very top floor, in one of
those large but tasteful executive offices intended to impress
but not overwhelm. The view was incredible, the appointments tasteful, the greeting from Ken warm and gracious. We
sat and talked about old times, who was where, what news we
had of old colleagues. He asked about my writing career, and I
asked about his latest position. As we talked, I was pleased to
see that he still had a youthful appearance about him, that
there was still a quiet energy in his eyes, that whatever this job
required, it gave back to him more than it took.

I mentioned something I had heard about him, the reverence with which he was held in the black community in New
York. He had, after all, gone where few other blacks had; his
accomplishments acquired a certain aura. A flicker went across

his eyes, so fast as to be unnoticeable. It was a personal re-action, but whatever it was that that statement meant to him, it was not for my consumption. He did not forget for a second who he was, who I was, what it would be prudent or appropri-ate to reveal. As I had always done with Ken, I saw him, in some way, as the road not taken, and I saw, in that instant, what it was that he had that I lacked. He was not only intimate with power — understood it, knew its uses and limits — but he had also comfortably married his talents to it. It was a marriage I had never been able to make. Something much more scruffy and less valued by American society had captured my allegiance, and once it had me, it had never let go.

After I left my meeting with Ken, I strolled through the elegant lobby of the building. The grand look of the place brought back to me how much fun it had once been to come to a place that looked like this, how easy it had been to be seduced by the thought that the grandeur was a reflection of the people who worked here. As I'd listened to Ken talk a little about his job, I could imagine every detail that went with this life, and could still feel its attractions. At the same time, I now knew that it was not the life that had been laid out for me. In fact, as I left and we shook hands, vowing to keep in touch, as I hoped we would, I knew that the end of my story was not even here, that it had already happened several years earlier.

It had been April 1994. The event was a party for the publication of my first novel, *These Same Long Bones*, held in the headquarters of the North Carolina Mutual in Durham. When I had told my publicist that I wanted to start my book tour in Durham, she had agreed, I think, a trifle reluctantly. I remember her asking me if I still knew people in Durham, if anyone would show up. I tried to explain how it was in a community like this one. Everyone would be there because it was an event, and no one wanted to be left out of an event, I told her. The reception took place in what was called the Heritage Room of the Mutual. All around the room were sepia-colored photographs of the people who had made the Mutual, who had given of themselves to create it. Everyone I knew or had ever known as a child in Durham came to the party — cousins, aunts, uncles, great-uncles, great-aunts. One of my cousins introduced me at the podium, reciting my list of accomplishments, and ending with how we had all known that Gwennie Mac would go far. I took the podium and, much to my surprise, was not nervous at all.

As I looked out at the faces looking up at mine — all of my family, so many friends — I realized that I had waited all my life to be here. My book told the story of a man who must find himself to save his community, who faces tragedy, the death of his only child, and must learn to transcend it. It was set in Durham, North Carolina, among a community of people not unlike those I now faced.

I began to speak.

"This community," I said, "has given me all that I know." I looked from face to face. This one was a face that had told me about grief. This one about loyalty, and betrayal. This one about courage and grace and faith. "It was here among you that I got my first taste of life, a sense of possibility, a sense of responsibility. I wrote this book as an homage to you."

Later I signed the books, to Cousin This and Cousin That, as everyone told me how we were related.

"I'm your father's cousin on your great-grandfather's side. Just sign it 'To Cousin Betty-Lu.'"

I signed and I signed and I signed. I laughed and lapsed into a Southern accent again. People took pictures with me and threw their arms around my shoulder or gave me a hug. "You haven't changed a bit, Gwennie Mac," they told me. "After all these years, you look just the same."

I briefly tried to imagine how I must look. My hair in braids again, not pigtails but something called Senegalese twists, flecked with silver. My head cocked to the side, as it usually is when I am thinking. My eyes shining almost too brightly, betraying my excitement. I was looking up at people with a broad smile, my pen poised in the air. I was related to these people not only by birth and tradition, but had been bequeathed a legacy of values as solid as a chestnut, rich with wisdom painted brown. I was ready now to speak of what I'd learned.